Understanding
Speaking in Tongues

Understanding Speaking in Tongues

By Watson E. Mills

William B. Eerdmans Publishing Company
Grand Rapids, Michigan

To my wife Joyce and my son Michael,
who bring meaning to this and all my endeavors.

CONTENTS

PREFACE

Utterance with tongues is the speech of angels in which the secrets of the heavenly world are revealed.

Wilhelm Bousset

In the midst of a charismatic revival, the church today finds herself facing new and pressing problems. The Pandora's box that is being opened throughout Christendom contains a multi-faceted variety of such phenomena as spiritualism, mental telepathy, mysticism, and the occult. Certainly a significant recent development has been the phenomenal rise of glossolalia. One researcher maintains that in America alone over three million people will have this experience in the twentieth century, while *Time* magazine describes glossolalia as one of the fastest growing fads in U.S. Protestant churches.

Thus it was with a sense of urgency that I began this critical research and evaluation. I have tried hard to achieve some degree of objectivity in my examination of this highly emotive subject — one about which people tend to be rather fiercely opinionated. The basic question to which I address myself here is at once simple and yet far reaching: What is the significance of glossolalia for the Christian who has *not* experienced the phenomenon? Or, as a non-glossolaliac, how do I relate to my brother who is having the experience of tongues? These kinds of questions are obviously significant for Christian unity.

I have tried to approach the subject in a spirit of intellectual honesty and Christian love, which is exceedingly difficult but, I believe, not impossible. The role of a detached critic is never easy, but is in this instance necessary if there is to be understanding between those who participate and those who do not.

So many people have rendered so much valuable assistance to me in preparing this manuscript that I cannot begin to show my gratitude. I must especially thank the faculty of the Southern Baptist Theological Seminary, where I undertook to write a doctoral dissertation in this area. My graduate studies' committee as well as the library staff helped in countless ways. But certainly no one has worked harder or more diligently than Miss Phyllis Rowland, who prepared the final draft, and Miss Pauline Coll, who helped in proofreading. It is impossible to praise their work too highly.

WATSON E. MILLS

Danville, Virginia

CHAPTER ONE

INTRODUCTION

My Non-Intelligence of Human Words
Ten Thousand Pleasures unto Me affords.

Thomas Traherne

A. What Is Glossolalia?

Two students from an Eastern and so-called "liberal" seminary were several miles from the stately sanctuary where they regularly worshipped. Acting partly out of curiosity but also out of intellectual arrogance, they strolled into a church that was not their standard fare at all. In fact, the Pentecostal church they entered was not the least socialistic, intellectual, or upper-class, let alone ecumenical. The service was a farce, they thought as they politely concealed their amusement. Yet ironically, as the service wore on, one of the two visitors experienced what he called in retrospect "a second baptism." Several months later this same young man spoke in tongues. But his companion at this service experienced nothing; in fact, he rejected not only his former friend but the entire tongues movement as well.

These two seminarians represent in microcosm what is happening throughout Christendom as the tongues movement reaches new heights of influence and prominence. That is, few Christians are indifferent toward glossolalia: either they have had the experience and regard it as central, or they flatly reject both the experience and the person who claims it. The movement has been referred to by its critics as "praying in gibberish," "fluent nonsense," "heresy in embryo," "esoteric self-indulgence" and "ecstatic ejaculation." One interpreter flatly states that "God does not deal in trivialities, obscurities, and unintelligible gibberish."[1] A spokesman for a sizeable denomination in the northwest said this: "Glossolalia generally has drawn people into a wilderness of idiosyncrasy whose only harvest has been briers; it tends to make for spiritual snobbery."[2] If name-calling does not discourage the glossolaliac, a given congregation may freeze him out through a calculated ostracism.

Yet those who are caught up in the tongues movement are equally vehement. Speaking in tongues is described, for example, as an "extraordinary gift," a "second blessing," "the only genuine manifestation of the Spirit." A Yale student likened it to "driving a nitroglycerine truck down a dirt road." Another glossolaliac reportedly remarked: "I saw praying hands grab the Holy power of God in a most supernatural way. . . . I saw God's men and women, boys and girls, saturated in the flaming power of the Holy Spirit."[3]

It is apparent that communication between the glossolaliac and the non-glossolaliac is strained, if present at all. And from every indication, the breach is widening. Already, countless numbers of people have been hurt, as have entire denominations. The Christian faith is being shaken to its foundations. It is time that each of us invests the effort to become carefully informed about this crucial issue.

[1]Stuart Bergsma, *Speaking with Tongues* (Grand Rapids: Baker, 1965), p. 24.

[2]Quoted in Donovan Bess, " 'Speaking in Tongues' — the High Church Heresy," *Nation*, CXCVII (1962), 175.

[3]Quoted in *Methodists and the Baptism of the Holy Spirit* (Los Angeles: Full Gospel Business Men's Fellowship International, 1963), p. 22.

B. Definition

"Glossolalia" is an English word compounded of the two Greek words *glossa* and *lalein*. In its hybrid form the term literally means "to speak in tongues." In common usage the term refers to the spontaneous utterance of uncomprehended and seemingly random vocal sounds. More precisely, the speech has been defined as "an effortless flow of usually complex structure, with the repetition and inflection characteristic of language."[4] In practice, the speech may sound quite like a chant or calypso singing. One researcher compiled some instances of the phenomenon. Here is one example:

> Ah 'ach ma hah moora, ay
> andorra ay ach-ah ha moora.
> Almtee muhr ah hah melah, ay
> ah nahah mahah murch
> mahlan.[5]

While the speech often contains inflections characteristic of a language, most linguists consistently maintain that the samples of glossolalia studied do not correspond to any language known to mankind. Eugene A. Nida of the American Bible Society conducted an analysis of "tongues" that were recorded on tape. He was assisted by specialists who represented more than 150 aboriginal languages in twenty-five different countries. Nida concluded that there was no resemblance to any actual language which has ever been treated by linguists. Communication, then, if present at all, obviously occurs on a deep psychological level and thus is not contingent upon the identification of the glossolalia with some specific language of mankind.

---

[4] Morton T. Kelsey, *Tongue Speaking: An Experiment in Spiritual Experience* (Garden City, New York: Doubleday, 1964), p. 1.

[5] Bess, p. 174.

C. Origin

Speaking in tongues is clearly referred to in the New Testament. Here, it appears to have evolved out of the desire of religious converts and devotees to have some specific, objective proof of their being possessed by the Spirit of God. Evidently glossolalia was accepted as unquestionable evidence.

At Pentecost, a soul-stirring experience dynamically affected the lives of those converts who were expecting some significant revelation from God. Consequently, a number of those present broke forth spontaneously into ecstatic speech. To many in the crowd they appeared drunk. For the converts it was a manifestation of the inflowing of the divine Spirit — the Spirit of power. Paul maintained that the Spirit was supposed to reveal his presence in the believer's life through special gifts (I Cor. 12:10; 12:28-31), and among these he lists speaking in tongues.

It is significant that, according to the biblical record, these random vocal sounds were addressed to God. Luke indicates that men were heard speaking in tongues and extolling God (Acts 10:46), and Paul notes that one who speaks in a tongue speaks not to men but to God (I Cor. 14:2). Thus it is possible that glossolalia was not intended to convey a message to men; rather, it was a form of prayer, as indicated in I Corinthians 14:14 and 14:16. It was an effort to express to God the inexpressible: the indwelling of his Spirit. That is, when the truth of God's revelation sank home to a responsive heart, ordinary conventional language was too restrictive to express the depth of the emotions that were aroused; consequently, the convert broke forth in ecstatic speech. It was essentially, then, an objective witness to the presence of the Spirit of God.

D. Effects

While its supporters point to the great blessings of tongue-speaking, its opponents argue that disunity and factionalism inevitably follow in its wake. Denominational leaders have not known what to do with the movement, since within the ranks of most major groups are those who support and those who oppose tongues. If the movement were an isolated occurrence with neither biblical nor historical justification, it would be a simple matter for Christendom to relegate the practice to the rear ranks. But such is not the case, since both the biblical narrative and church history make it impossible to deny the phenomenon. Indeed, the apostle Paul claims to have experienced it himself: "I thank God that I speak in tongues more than you all. . ." (I Cor. 14:18).

Everywhere in Christendom the results seem to be the same. For the person who speaks in tongues it is a meaningful spiritual experience. But for the non-glossolaliac the phenomenon brings divisiveness, emotionalism, and a disregard for the ordered, sacramental theology of the church. So it is that while some Christians want to cultivate the gift of tongues because it is the much-to-be-desired signal of charismatic revival, others with equal vigor would avoid it as nothing more than an escape from the more costly demands of the Christian faith. Unsympathetic estimates of the significance of glossolalia reflect a degree of impatience and immaturity on the part of the critics that is not substantially different from that which they so readily attribute to the glossolaliacs.

As could be expected, many have suffered already because of a genuine lack of understanding of this complex problem. Both those who foster tongue-speaking and those who vehemently oppose it are often found wanting of carefully informed opinions about this highly emotive subject. This kind of atmosphere breeds rash reactions that can ultimately only damage the church and weaken the charismatic revival many are heralding.

E. A Brief History of the Movement

While there have been scattered instances of glossolalia throughout the history of the Christian church, it was not until the late seventeenth century that the phenomenon occurred among numerous people of one locality. In southern France, the Cevenols, who lived under the strain of severe persecution, had ecstatic experiences that included speaking in tongues. In the nineteenth century a second major outburst of tongue-speaking occurred in England. The followers of the movement, known as Irvingites, gathered around the Scottish Presbyterian pastor Edward Irving, though strangely enough he himself never received the gift of glossolalia.

Several Pentecostal revivals sprang up in the United States just after the turn of the twentieth century. The earliest recorded instance of glossolalia in this century was in Topeka, Kansas, in 1901, when the "baptism of the Spirit" fell upon Miss Agnes N. Ozman, a student at the Bethel Bible College.[6] From Kansas the movement spread to Missouri and Texas. By 1906, tongue-speaking was being practiced as far away as Los Angeles. Here "the movement began to take on international proportions"[7] with the birth of twenty-six new churches, numbering a total of over two million members.[8]

In the last decade glossolalia has also made great gains among the non-Pentecostal groups. On April 3, 1960, Reverend Dennis J. Bennett confessed a belief in tongue-speaking from the pulpit of his Van Nuys, California, Episcopalian church. He said that "the Holy Spirit did take my lips and tongue and form a new and powerful language of praise and prayer that I myself could not understand...."[9] This was the first reported public incident of glossolalia among the so-called non-Pentecostal denominations, and it signaled the debut of a phenomenon which undoubtedly had existed for some years in private.

---

[6] Robert Chandler Dalton, *Tongues Like As of Fire: A Critical Study of the Modern Tongue Movement in the Light of Apostolic and Patristic Times* (Springfield, Missouri: Gospel Publishing House, 1945), p. 31.

[7] E. Glenn Hinson, "A Brief History of Glossolalia," in Frank Stagg, E. Glenn Hinson, and Wayne E. Oates, *Glossolalia: Tongue Speaking in Biblical, Historical and Psychological Perspective* (Nashville: Abingdon, 1967), p. 69.

[8] Kelsey, p. 64.

[9] Bess, p. 173.

Four years later, the American Lutheran Church Council voted to relieve Reverend A. Herbert Mjorud from the church's evangelical staff. His offense, as reported in *Time* magazine, was one "that appalls, embarrasses and deeply worries church leaders: promoting glossolalia, the practice of praying in 'gibberish.' "[10] These were not isolated cases: by 1964 only one Lutheran pastor in Montana had not spoken in tongues.

Many laymen have also become involved in the movement. M. G. (Pat) Robertson, son of former Virginia Senator A. Willis Robertson, is a glossolaliac. He plans to expand his Christian television station into a Christian Broadcasting Network as a result of his vivid experience of speaking in tongues.[11]

Intellectual sophistication strengthens the thrust of the movement, as men like Bennett, Harald Bredesen (a Reformed minister), and Larry Christenson (an American Lutheran pastor) relate their own experiences of tongue-speaking. *Time* magazine reported that twenty young people from Yale University had experienced the phenomenon, and indicated that these students

> are far from being Holy Rollers. One is a Roman Catholic, and most of the others are Protestants who belong to the sober-sided Inter-Varsity Christian Fellowship — Episcopalians, Lutherans, Presbyterians, and Methodists.[12]

At Princeton Seminary, fifty-five students were involved in prayer groups where many spoke in tongues. The movement spread from Princeton to more than twenty colleges and seminaries. In fact, the movement is so significant on the college level that Marcus Bach devoted a major section of his book *The Inner Ecstasy* to the phenomenon, exploring tongues from the students' perspective.

[10] "Taming the Tongues," *Time,* LXXXIV (July 10, 1964), 64.

[11] M. G. Robertson, "Directed of the Lord," in *Baptists and the Baptism of the Holy Spirit,* ed. Jerry Jensen (Los Angeles: Full Gospel Business Men's Fellowship International, n.d.), pp. 24-26.

[12] "Worship: Blue Tongues," *Time,* LXXXI (March 29, 1963), 52.

The movement has been given a considerable boost by the Full Gospel Business Men's Fellowship International, which was founded in 1953 by a group of Pentecostals, but whose membership now includes virtually all denominations. In 1959 this organization began publishing a periodical entitled *View*.

Another organization particularly interested in glossolalia is the Blessed Trinity Society of Van Nuys, California, which was started by Episcopalians. Between 1962 and 1966 it published a handsome slick magazine entitled *Trinity* which was distributed among the historic denominations. It carried testimonials that were aimed at proving tongues to be more than just another religious fad.

But by far the most common groups in which tongue-speech flourishes are the small Holy Spirit Fellowships that have sprung up throughout Christendom. Usually these groups are small and relatively unstructured. Along with speaking in tongues, they often have prayer, testimonials, and singing.

F. Significance of Glossolalia

Only a few years ago it was possible to dismiss the tongues movement as belonging to the various ultra-fundamentalist denominations, composed largely of ignorant people who were highly emotional and basically unstable. But in more recent times, even the "respectable" denominations have become involved. This development was so astounding that one interpreter entitled his assessment of the situation "Tongues in Transition,"[13] while *The Nation* carried an article entitled "Speaking in Tongues — the High Church Heresy."[14] Another interpreter remarked caustically: "The breath of the living God is stirring among the dry bones of the major respectable, old established denominations."[15]

[13] J. D. Douglas, "Tongues in Transition," *Christianity Today*, X (July 8, 1966), 34.

[14] Bess, pp. 173-177.

[15] Quoted in Frank A. Tinker, "The Strange Words That Threaten Protestant Unity," *Pageant*, XX (June, 1965), 81.

As part of the larger movement that Russell Hitt, editor of *Eternity* magazine, calls "The New Pentecostalism,"[16] tongues supposedly signal the beginning of the end of secularism and a restoration of vital spontaneity into the main stream of a stagnant church.

But the question that looms for the nonparticipating Christian is this: what does all this tongue speech mean? How am I to relate to my brother who speaks in tongues? It is this crucial question that will be the concern of the following pages.

[16] Russell T. Hitt, "The New Pentecostalism: An Appraisal," *Eternity*, XIV (July, 1963), 10.

CHAPTER TWO

THE BACKGROUND OF CHRISTIAN GLOSSOLALIA

When my tongue is loosed most,
then most I lose my speech.

Henry Austin Dobson

Glossolalia is not an exclusively Christian phenomenon. Speaking in tongues was practiced for many years by the prophets of the ancient religions of the Near East. The practice is often seen in the larger context of ecstaticism, and once this assimilation is made, glossolalia takes its place in a long line of religious phenomena in which the devotee is given to such conditions as trances, hypnotic states, or extreme euphoria, followed or accompanied by such behavior as dancing, shouting, whirling, jerking, prostration, and speaking with tongues.

Because of the connection between glossolalia and ecstatic phenomena in general, a study of tongue-speaking should include a survey of the development of ecstaticism and its relationship to the Old Testament prophets, who are in the immediate background of the references to glossolalia in the New Testament. For not only does the Pentecost narrative center around members of the Jewish race, but it also quotes the prophet Joel.

It should be noted, however, that the discovery of similar phenomena in no sense proves any organic or psychic relationship to the Christian phenomenon of tongues. Rather, it simply attests to the general tendency of man to seek the aid of his god in varying degrees of persistence and intensity. Tongue-speech may be one instance of this basic reality.

A. Ecstaticism Outside the Old Testament

The Judeo-Christian tradition is obviously not solely responsible for the origin and perpetuation of ecstaticism. Historical evidence indicates that ecstaticism was indeed more of a universal phenomenon; in fact, the kind of frenzied speech that may be called glossolalia probably had its roots in the ancient religions of Asia Minor,[1] although there is no positive evidence. The earliest instance of an experience is found in the report of Wenamon, an Egyptian who journeyed through Palestine and Phoenicia about 1117 B.C. While in Byblos he wrote the following account:

> Now when he sacrificed to his gods, the god seized one of his noble youths, making him frenzied, so that he said: "Bring [the god] hither! Bring the messenger of Amon who hath him. Send him, and let him go."
>
> .... the frenzied [youth] continued in frenzy during this night.[2]

Two significant factors emerge from the report: (1) the report implies the youth is possessed by a god; (2) the youth's ecstatic speech contained at least some words that were understandable. At least in this case, then, ecstatic speech was not necessarily equivalent to unintelligible speech.

Again, near the end of the second millennium before Christ, a revival of the worship of Dionysus swept rapidly

---

[1]Carlyle L. May, "A Survey of Glossolalia and Related Phenomena in Non-Christian Religions," *American Anthropologist,* LVIII (February, 1956), 75.

[2]Cited in James Henry Breasted, *Ancient Records of Egypt,* 5 vols. (Chicago: University of Chicago, 1906), IV, 278.

over Greece and Syria-Palestine. The devotees experienced a kind of religious rapture or ecstasy much like intoxication. James Pratt compared the Dionysiac cult to " 'revival meetings' — and these of a very emotional and exciting sort."[3] Euripides, in his play *Bacchae,* tells how these Dionysiac worshippers longed for this ecstatic experience.

> Ah, shall my white feet in the dances gleam
> The livelong night again? Ah, shall I there
> Float through the Bacchanal's ecstatic dream,
> Tossing my neck in the dewy air?[4]

In light of this kind of evidence, W. F. Albright suggests that possibly Israelite ecstaticism was somewhat akin to the ecstatic frenzy of the Dionysiac worshippers. "The legendary Bacchantic eruption into Greece," he states, "of which Euripides wrote so eloquently, and the prophetic movement in Israel may have a common historical source."[5] It is credible both sociologically and psychologically that the ecstaticism of the early Yahwists grew out of the same general religious milieu that produced the Dionysiac worshippers, although it is evident that the ecstaticism associated with Yahwism followed a radically different line of development from the eleventh century B.C.[6]

B. Ecstaticism in the Old Testament

The trail of the historical appearances of ecstaticism leads directly to the Old Testament. Canaanite religion may have been the medium through which the movement was introduced into the religious life of the Israelites. Thus, some interpreters argue, ecstatic forms of prophecy were native to Canaanite rather than Hebrew culture.

---

[3]James B. Pratt, *The Religious Consciousness* (New York: Macmillan, 1937), p. 167.

[4]Euripides, *Bacchae,* in *The Complete Greek Drama,* ed. Whitney J. Oates and Eugene O'Neill, 2 vols. (New York: Random, 1938), II, 260.

[5]William Foxwell Albright, *From the Stone Age to Christianity* (Baltimore: Johns Hopkins, 1946), p. 305.

[6]Wayne E. Oates, "Ecstaticism" (unpublished seminar paper, Duke University, Durham, North Carolina, 1943), p. 3.

While the first reference to the ecstatic is found in Numbers 11:24-29, the earliest *detailed* examples of the phenomenon in the Hebraic tradition are to be found among the prophets. In fact, there is no reason to doubt the existence of bands of ecstatic prophets as late as the time of David.[7] Some of these roving bands were no doubt considered to be inspired by the Spirit. A central passage for ascertaining the nature of this inspiration is found in I Samuel:

> . . . you will meet a band of prophets coming down from the high place with harp, tambourine, flute, and lyre before them, prophesying. Then the spirit of the Lord will come mightily upon you, and you shall prophesy with them and be turned into another man. (I Sam. 10:5b-6)

It is assumed that the Hebrew people first encountered the phenomenon at the time of the conquest and settlement of Canaan. In confronting the ecstatic phenomena of the land of Canaan, the Israelites were first introduced to a form of manticism (madness) that produced a supernatural change in the personality of the prophet and effectively united him to the divine, which then entered into him and used his vocal organs.[8] But succeeding generations became so suspicious of the ecstatic form of prophecy that the prophet was considered "mad," and the prophet of the eighth century did not hesitate to say so (Hos. 9:7; Jer. 29:26. Cf. II Kings 9:11). Whatever influence of the later prophetic movement can be seen in the Numbers' account of Eldad and Medad was most likely written into it later by those who distrusted ecstatic prophecy.

There are important differences between the Israelite notion of prophetic consciousness and that of their pagan neighbors. According to Canaanite interpretation, for example, the prophet was seized by the god, whose spokesman he became, so that the prophet became identified with that god. This deification of the human was assuredly

---

[7]Gerhard von Rad, *Old Testament Theology*, trans. D. M. G. Stalker, 2 vols. (Edinburgh: Oliver and Boyd, 1965), II, 10.

[8]Harold Knight, *The Hebrew Prophetic Consciousness* (London: Lutterworth, 1947), p. 52.

21

most repugnant to the Hebrews, who resolutely insisted upon the vast distance which existed between God and his prophet.

External patterns of behavior, such as incoherent speech, insensibility to pain, wild leaping and contortions, and abnormal expressions,[9] were manifested in the ecstasy of both the Hebrew and Canaanite. It would have been easy, therefore, for the two to merge into a kind of syncretistic form in subsequent generations; and such may have been the case. So the Hebrew prophet could not and would not escape the ecstatic phenomena; yet he added to these a new significance by interpreting them in light of his own psychology and theology.[10]

According to this interpretation, a reaction of true prophetic enthusiasm developed among the Hebrews against the mystical-ecstatic forms of Canaanite culture. This does not mean, however, that a rigid distinction between the "cultic" and the "canonical" prophets resulted. On the contrary, there were definitely ecstatic features among the writing prophets.[11] The difference lay in the fact that there was a continuous, gradual, but definite, development away from ecstatic forms of prophecy toward a more ordered form of discourse.[12]

Hosea notes that "the prophet is a fool, the man of the spirit is mad" (Hos. 9:7b), while Jeremiah writes:

> The Lord has made you priest instead of Jehoiada the priest, to have charge in the house of the Lord over every madman who prophesies, to put him in the stocks and collar. (Jer. 29:26)

We see developing, then, a higher standard by which to evaluate Spirit possession — no longer are ecstatic mani-

[9]Theodore H. Robinson, *Prophecy and the Prophets* (London: Duckworth, 1950), pp. 30-31.

[10]Knight, p. 53.

[11]For example, Ezekiel's psychic transports (Ezek. 3:14; 11:5; 11:13; 37:1-10); Jeremiah's emotional outbursts (Jer. 4:19; 8:18; 9:1; 10:19-20); Isaiah's vision in the temple (Isa. 6:1-13).

[12]H. Wheeler Robinson, *Inspiration and Revelation in the Old Testament* (Oxford: Clarendon, 1946), p. 175.

festations the sole criterion. Frenzied speech did not of itself guarantee possession by the Spirit.

C. Ecstaticism in the Inter-Biblical Period

During the inter-testamental period there are only a few references to ecstatic speaking among the Jews. One example is found in the apocryphal book of II Esdras, where Ezra offers the following account of an ecstatic experience:

> Then I opened my mouth, and behold, a full cup was offered to me; it was full of something like water, but its color was like fire. And I took it and drank; and when I had drunk it, my heart poured forth understanding, and wisdom increased in my breast, for my spirit retained its memory; and my mouth was opened, and was no longer closed. (II Esdras 14:39-41)

It appears that Ezra induced his experience through drugs. Amanuenses attended him during the episode to record the "sacred" words which would flow from his frenzied lips. Unless we assume that the amanuenses had a "gift of interpretation," we must conclude that Ezra spoke in a perfectly comprehensible manner.

Though admittedly an argument from silence, it seems reasonable to conclude that since the inter-biblical records so largely disregard the phenomenon, ecstatic speech enjoyed little popularity as the means of expressing the indwelling of the Spirit during these years.

D. Ecstaticism in the First Century

Contrary to the conclusions of many modern writers, it is not easy to establish the existence of parallels to glossolalia among the religions of the first century. The sources dating from the first and second centuries of the Christian era — for example, Strabo, Plutarch, and Pausanias — indicate that the oracles may have been expressed in an *intelligible*, though difficult, language, and that thus there may not be any basis for comparing these with glossolalia.

The oracle at Delphi was the most famous in the ancient world. Strabo indicates that she received the "breath" that inspired a "divine frenzy" and then uttered oracles in both verse and prose.[13] In addition, Plutarch refers to the emotional frenzy of the mystery religions. He quotes Herodotus regarding the rites of these groups. There was "frenzy and shouting of throngs in excitement with tumultuous tossing of heads in the air."[14] Strabo offers an account of the whirling of cymbals and clicking of castanets that were used in the worship of Dionysus, Cybele, and others.[15] He also describes the shouts of "ev-ah" and the stamping of feet that produced a religious frenzy.[16] In these instances, the emphasis seems to be upon manifestations of ecstasy other than unintelligible speech. While the accounts mention ecstatic phenomena, they stop short of specifying unintelligible speech.

E. Conclusion

On the basis of the records, it seems logical to recognize that ecstatic, frenzied speech did exist prior to the Christian era, but it is too hypothetical to postulate that this speech was the same as that in Acts and I Corinthians. It appears that the Greeks were ecstatic, but that their speech was not always unintelligible. This means that in the Graeco-Roman world contemporary to the early church frenzied speech in a religious context was not extraordinary but rather commonplace. It means that the early Christians may well have known of a religious phenomenon not wholly different from what occurred on Pentecost.

The total impression one gets when surveying the instances of ecstaticism is that the apostolic phenomenon of

---

[13]Strabo, *Geography*, IX, iii, 5, in *The Geography of Strabo*, trans. Horace Leonard Jones, 8 vols., The Loeb Classical Library (London: Heinemann, 1927-1932), IV, 353.

[14]Plutarch, *The Obsolescence of Oracles*, XIV, in *Plutarch's Moralia*, trans. Frank Cole Babbitt, 10 vols., The Loeb Classical Library (London: Heinemann, 1944-1949), V, 391.

[15]Strabo, *Geography*, X, iii, 13, in Jones, V, 99-101.

[16]*Ibid.*

glossolalia was not a unique event in the history of religious experience. The world-view of the Greeks and Romans was tolerant of these frenzied, ecstatic utterances. Such occurrences attest to the fact that mankind has always longed for God to be on his side and to invest him with divine power. This desire inevitably leads to some type of objective expression whereby the internal power of God may be demonstrated. Certainly, ecstatic speech was one such expression; however, one should not make the mistake of linking earlier appearances of ecstaticism into a lineal descent which leads ultimately to the New Testament church. The most that can be said is that these isolated instances of ecstaticism indicate the presence of frenzied speech *in a religious* context and indicate a religious *milieu* in which ecstaticism was readily acceptable, though not necessarily approved. There is some evidence, however, that by the first century, objective phenomena intended to prove the indwelling of the Spirit were suspect. These phenomena were even considered manifestations of an evil spirit.

CHAPTER THREE

TONGUES IN ACTS

Death and life are in the power of the tongue . . . .
                                                    Proverbs 18:21

Someone once remarked that every word has its own personality, "a translation is but a mask." This is precisely the case with the word "tongue" in the Bible. Its meanings are many and diverse, but none is so hotly debated as the meaning of the expression "speaking in tongues." The purpose of this chapter is to examine speaking in tongues in the book of Acts.

A. The Biblical Usages of "Tongue"

There is no single Greek word underlying the English term "glossolalia," although the phrase "to speak with tongues" does occur in Mark 16:17 and Acts 2:4. There are frequent occurrences of the word "tongue" *(glossa)* in several different senses in the New Testament: (1) as an organ of taste and speech, as in Luke 1:64 and 16:24; (2) as a synonym for "people" or "nation," as in Revelation 5:9, 7:9, 10:11, and 14:6; (3) to describe a tongue-like shape, as in the "tongues as of fire" referred to in Acts 2:3; (4) for obscure or very strange speech, as in I Corinthians 12-14 and Acts 2:4, 10:46, and 19:6. This "strange" speech is now commonly referred to as "glosso-lalia," or "speaking in tongues," and is by far the most problematic usage.

Since the only explicit New Testament references to what is now termed glossolalia occur in Acts and I Corinthians — Mark 16:17 is generally recognized as a late addition to Mark and not part of the original text, and thus is disregarded here — it is necessary now to discuss these two books in detail with reference to the phenomenon of speaking in tongues.

B. The Lukan Concept of the Spirit

As in his gospel, so in Acts, Luke's purpose is to proclaim that salvation is in Jesus Christ; indeed, salvation was the burden of apostolic preaching in general. It was this factor that brought about the Jerusalem conference: "But some men came down from Judea and were teaching the brethren, 'Unless you are circumcised according to the custom of Moses, you cannot be saved' " (Acts 15:1).

Granted Luke's keen interest in the salvation motif, a logical postulate is that the concept of witness is also central to his writing. Many of the speeches betray the witness motif: Acts 2:32; 3:15; 5:32; 13:31; 20:21; 26:16. Indeed, the first chapter of the book projects the idea of witness and emphasizes that there are those especially commissioned to be witnesses.

Just as surely as Luke's intention was to proclaim God's salvation and to witness to that reality, so he was convinced that the witness of the Holy Spirit was the ultimate validation of that salvation. Luke carefully shows how at every milepost along the route of salvation history, the Spirit of God was in evidence: at the beginning in Jerusalem, during the expansion in Judea and the invasion of Samaria, in the introduction of the gospel to the gentiles at Caesarea and Ephesus, and especially in the life and ministry of Paul, who was the symbolic instrument of the outreach of the gospel to the ends of the earth.

In his gospel, Luke stresses how the initial steps of Jesus' ministry are marked by the *power* of the Spirit —

for example, in Jesus' confrontation with the devil. Subtly, Luke equates "power" with "Spirit." Furthermore, at several points Luke intimates that the Spirit will be made available to all Christians at some point in the future. These intimations become very explicit in the final chapter of his gospel, when Jesus assures the disciples that they will be clothed with power from above. This promise may be viewed as a link between the gospel and Acts, since the promise is reiterated in the opening verses of Acts. Then in the second chapter of Acts, the promise becomes a reality. It is on the day of Pentecost that the disciples finally realize the fruition of Jesus' promise.

It was a young Christian community empowered by the Spirit that would be the instrument through which would flow the proclamation of the gospel. In ever widening circles, the gospel would reach "to the ends of the earth." From Jerusalem and Judea through Samaria, no obstacle would hinder its progress. At significant mileposts along its difficult route, the Spirit of God would be present as if to insure divine approval.

C. The Importance of the Pentecost Narrative

The second chapter of Acts contains a relatively detailed account of the first Christian Pentecost, that is, of the first day of Pentecost after the crucifixion and resurrection of Jesus. According to the description given, a series of events took place at that time which added a uniquely Christian aspect to the ancient Jewish festival. The amount of space given to the happenings on that day, the position of prominence accorded to these events in relation to the book as a whole, and the striking contrast in the portrayal of the primitive Christian community before and after the first Pentecost — all these factors indicate the tremendous value Luke placed upon the occasion. Luke regards as preparatory to the experience itself some of the pre-Pentecost occurrences. For Luke, the Pentecost experience marks not only the outpouring of the Spirit but also the first in a series of great advances for the young gospel.

D. The Purpose of the Pentecost Narrative

The discussion of the role of the Spirit in Luke-Acts, as well as the importance of the Pentecost narrative within that framework, makes it obvious that in Luke's eyes the Spirit's role on the day of Pentecost was to bestow upon the apostles the *power* needed for the mission confronting them. In fact, the Spirit is that power.

Despite the difficulties for the modern mind, the amazing inbreak of supernatural power at Pentecost caused little or no surprise among the participants. Luke indicates in Acts 1:4-5 that they knew that this was the fulfillment of the Lord's repeated promise of fuller life and power. In addition, Peter's citation of Joel's prophecy indicates that the event was also seen as a renewal of the Old Testament gift of prophecy — in this case, however, not to a select few, but rather to all believers alike. It appears, then, that the primitive church was a society of people who believed themselves to have been given the very power of God himself through his Spirit. The various "abnormal" phenomena were symptoms attesting to the Spirit's invasion of their lives. From observable effects they deduced causes. The inevitable conclusion was that the same power which operated in and through the person of their Lord was now poured out upon them. Maurice Barnett correctly observes that "the abnormal features cannot be put aside as hysteria" because to the Hebrew mind "they were accompaniments of a stirring awakening."[1]

E. Interpreting Acts 2

The heart of the New Testament discussion of speaking in tongues is found in the Pentecost narrative in Acts, for the "gift of tongues" was given at the time the Holy Spirit was poured out upon the infant church.

Despite the various ways of regarding glossolalia, what Luke says in Acts 2 is really clear enough. In fact, most (though not all) interpreters believe that Luke represents

---

[1]Maurice Barnett, *The Living Flame* (London: Epworth, 1953), pp. 59-60.

the tongues on the day of Pentecost to have been under-standable languages of some kind. There is a miracle in-volved, according to Luke, either in the speaking or the hear-ing or perhaps both. Thus these Jewish pilgrims of various linguistic pedigrees could understand, each in his own na-tive language, what was being uttered by those upon whom the Spirit of God was descending. Luke emphasizes the understanding, but, unfortunately, does not tell us how this understanding was possible.

1. Traditional Interpretations

The details of glossolalia at Pentecost are not so clear as one might wish, and of the many problems presented by the account, none is more baffling than the reference to "other tongues" in Acts 2:4. Does the expression refer to other languages, as the eighth verse seems to indicate? Bib-lical interpreters take one of three positions in answer to this question.

(1) Some scholars hold that the tongues represent intel-ligible speech. The greater number of interpreters have understood the tongues to refer to foreign languages, either entirely or partly. The early church fathers, for example, commonly took this position. Irenaeus notes that there are "many brethren in the Church . . . who through the Spirit speak all kinds of languages. . . ."[2] Augustine observes: "Every one of them spoke in tongues of all na-tions; thus signifying that the unity of the catholic Church would embrace all nations, and would in like manner speak in all times."[3]

This theory has also enjoyed popularity in more recent years. Miles Smith, for example, dogmatically maintains that the Pentecost narrative will admit of no other inter-pretation.[4] Other scholars hold that while Luke might

[2]Irenaeus, *Against Heresies,* V, vi, 1, in *Ante-Nicene Fathers,* ed. Philip Schaff, 10 vols. (New York: Scribner's, 1908), I, 531.

[3]Augustine, *The City of God,* XVII, 49, in *Nicene and Post-Nicene Fathers*, ed. Philip Schaff, 14 vols. (Grand Rapids: Eerdmans, 1956), II, 391.

[4]Miles W. Smith, *On Whom the Spirit Came* (Philadelphia: Judson, 1948), p. 22.

have misunderstood the actual event, he clearly regards the tongues as utterances in foreign languages.[5]

Arthur Wright attempts to defend the interpretation of tongues as foreign languages by referring to the children of the Cevennes (1687-1701), who preached at length in acceptable French instead of their native dialect.[6] Wright explains the phenomenon by claiming that the children were simply repeating sermons they had heard earlier. Similarly, he argues, the Pentecost narrative merely attributes to the primitive Christians the ability to repeat what they had heard at earlier feasts. They contributed no distinctively Christian teachings, but rather recited the "mighty works of God" in many unknown languages.

Other scholars who maintain that the glossolalia at Pentecost was intelligible foreign speech consider that speech to have been intermittent rather than extended. Doremus Hayes, whose analysis is also a variant of Wright's theory, states that the apostles experienced a case of heightened memory as a result of the emotional experience at Pentecost, and thus were able to speak intermittently in foreign phrases they had heard earlier.[7]

Kirsopp Lake admits that the glossolalia at Pentecost was possibly interspersed with foreign words and phrases, but suggests that these were distinct from foreign languages in the usual sense. He concludes that the tradition of the foreign languages is but

> an attempt by a friendy editor, separated from the actual event, to explain the glossolalia, just as the charge of drunkenness was the attempt of unfriendly observers, separated by a lack of sympathy.[8]

[5]Barnett, p. 82.

[6]Arthur Wright, *Some New Testament Problems* (London: Methuen, 1898), p. 269.

[7]Doremus Almy Hayes, *The Gift of Tongues* (Cincinnati: Jennings and Graham, 1913), pp. 60-61.

[8]F. J. Foakes-Jackson and Kirsopp Lake, *The Beginnings of Christianity: The Acts of the Apostles*, 5 vols. (New York: Macmillan, 1920-1933), V, 120.

(2) Another group of scholars maintains the Pentecost narrative represents not a miracle of speech, but one of hearing. George Cutten, for example, argues that the speech itself was unintelligible to the ordinary hearer, but that the gift of the Spirit issued in understanding.[9] Obviously this attaches considerable importance to the fact that verse 8 states that the spectators *heard* in their native language, not that the *speaking* was in their native language.

This interpretation argues that there seem to be two groups in the crowd — the "devout men" and the "others" who mock. It is the former group of pious men who understand the glossolalia as their "own native language," not the critical mockers. But although this theory of the Pentecostal experience is highly attractive, it does raise certain problems.

First, a division of the crowd into two groups is not really warranted by the narrative itself. On the contrary, it is natural to assume that all diaspora Jews who would gather in Jerusalem for the feast might be called "devout" men. Moreover, Luke gives the impression that *everyone* heard in his own language.

Then too, the narrative itself does not suggest that Luke thought any miracle was connected with the hearing of the glossolalia. He does not indicate that the gift of the Spirit descended upon the crowd. Nor does he mention any interpreting or translating taking place. And it is highly unlikely that any detached observer who was not himself caught up in the apostolic band would presume to interpret what was being said.

Finally, it appears that Luke, in fact, emphasizes the speaking and not the hearing. He indicates in verses 6 and 8 that this speech was being uttered even before the crowd had assembled. According to the narrative, it may even have been *because* the Jews recognized their native dialects that they gathered.

---

[9]George B. Cutten, *Speaking with Tongues: Historically and Psychologically Considered* (New Haven: Yale University, 1927), *passim.*

(3) A third group of scholars asserts that the Pentecost narrative is actually invalid, and that if indeed there was such a phenomenon as glossolalia, it was totally unintelligible. The logical end of this position is to affirm that the original text has become corrupted, or simply that the event itself is a fabrication.

Maurice Goguel is representative. He contends that the Jerusalem church was nonpneumatic in its nature and that pneumatism was peculiar to Greek Christianity.[10] Since the event of Pentecost happened before the author's time, he was forced to form his own idea of what glossolalia meant, and in doing so he not only misunderstood the phenomena but imposed a Greek mentality on the Jerusalem church.

Some critics regard Luke's record as the conflation of two or more sources. Adolf von Harnack, for example, holds Acts 3:1 through 5:16 to be the primitive narrative, while relegating Acts 2 and 5:17-42 to the role of a legendary recension of the same events.[11] This "doublet theory" has attracted much attention, but though it certainly represents an ingenious bit of scholarship, it has not been widely accepted among New Testament interpreters.

2. An Evaluation

The interpretive difficulties presented by St. Luke's account of the Pentecostal gift of tongues may be summarized as follows:

(1) Nowhere else in the New Testament is glossolalia understood as the ability to speak in foreign languages. Although Paul, for the sake of illustration, compares the tongues at Corinth with foreign languages, his basic contention is that no one is able to understand them. This position, then, runs counter to any interpretation of Acts 2 which holds that the men present from "every nation under heaven" *could* understand the Pentecostal glos-

---

[10]Maurice Goguel, *The Birth of Christianity*, trans. H. C. Snape (New York: Macmillan, 1954), pp. 95ff.

[11]Adolf von Harnack, *The Acts of the Apostles*, trans. J. R. Wilkerson (New York: Putnam's, 1909), pp. 179-183, 188-189.

solalia. Furthermore, the author of Acts himself records other instances of glossolalia (Acts 10:46; 19:6), and in neither of these is it stated or implied that foreign languages were involved.

(2) Even the Pentecost narrative itself does not consistently maintain that a miracle of foreign languages occurred. Some of those present said, "They are filled with new wine." This is not the impression that foreign languages would have made. Further, when Peter begins to preach, he takes his start from the accusation of drunkenness, and he never mentions foreign languages. His introduction presupposes that everyone has *not* understood what was said.

(3) There are indications that suggest that the canonical record of the Pentecost event may have been edited or conflated. The catalog of nations does not include "every nation under heaven" — the Greek homelands of Macedonia and Achaia are conspicuously missing. Nor is it likely that Jews living in those various places would know the ancient local dialects, since either Aramaic or Greek was the common language of the people in all those places named.

In the face of these difficulties, scholars who forego the foreign language motif propose several ultimate solutions:

(1) Heinrich Weinel[12] maintains that Acts was written so late that the author was no longer familiar with the actual details of the event. Unable to understand his source, he invented the explanation of foreign languages.

(2) E. F. Scott[13] acknowledges that Luke was quite familiar with glossolalia as it occurred in the early church, but argues that in this instance he was carried away by his love for symbolism. Scott cites the rejection at Nazareth (Luke 4:16-30) as an expression of an historical event dressed out by Luke's imagination to serve as a frontis-

[12]Heinrich Weinel, *Die Wirkungen des Geistes und der Geister im nachapostolischen Zeitalter bis auf Irenaüs* (Freiburg: Mohr, 1899), pp. 74ff.

[13]Ernest F. Scott, *The Spirit in the New Testament* (New York: Doran, 1923), p. 96.

piece for his gospel, signalizing the ultimate rejection of Jesus by his own people. Similarly, the Pentecost narrative has been dressed out as the frontispiece of Acts, to signify the ultimate reception of the gospel by men of all nations.

(3) The other possible solution is that there has been an interpolation into an originally self-consistent narrative. Luke may or may not have made this interpolation. For the moment, let the reader assume that Luke or a later editor did in fact insert the foreign language motif into the Pentecost narrative (possible explanations for such an action will be discussed below). With this assumption, quite apart from the question of intelligibility or unintelligibility, in terms of strict language communication it would now be possible to assess the Pentecost narrative for *meaning*. If it is possible to hold in abeyance the question of foreign languages, it will be feasible to move ahead to the larger problem of grasping the *meaning* of glossolalia regardless of its external, formal structure. It may well be that the understanding of glossolalia is tied to Luke's purpose and reason for incorporating the Pentecost narrative into the book of Acts.

3. A Reconstruction

The foregoing considerations urge us to search elsewhere for an understanding of the meaning of the glossolalia at Pentecost. It may well be that the significance of glossolalia is tied to Luke's reason for incorporating the Pentecost narrative into the book of Acts. I should like to suggest that the theological intent of Acts, in the final analysis, is to demonstrate that the gospel is dependent neither upon Peter nor Paul, nor the twelve, but rather upon a superhuman power — the Spirit of God. Furthermore, it seems clear that, in the light of its background in the Old Testament and its role in the early church, the Spirit was not something that welled up within man, as a part of his natural endowment. Rather, it was the ineffable "something" external to man that transcended his existence and touched him to the very depths of his being. Thus it appears that scholarship may be on an irrelevant track when it limits its understanding of glossolalia primarily to whether or not it was indeed a foreign language. Even if this question could be settled positively, there would remain unanswered the larger — and more central — question of *meaning*. In the light of the criticisms discussed above, however, it would appear valid to assume that the glossolalia of Pentecost should not be understood *simply* as foreign languages, though it may be this: the main consideration is that one not lose sight of that force which turned this unique phenomenon into a meaningful event. In Luke's eyes this force was none other than the Spirit of God. It was he who empowered the apostles for the missionary work of the gospel, he who supported them in their preaching, and he who was the chief witness of the truth of the gospel.[14]

It is therefore not the case that the author of Acts had a "naive interest in the miraculous" or in the abnormal psychic phenomena attending the Spirit's working, but rather, since these manifestations are the natural accompaniment of the Spirit, he simply sought to report the workings of the Spirit in their context. Of the abnormal manifestations enumerated in Acts, the special speech phenomena took first place. While glossolalia was neither properly didactic nor properly practical, there was, no doubt, some kind of communication within the context of the community.

Certainly, intelligible language is not always necessary for communication and understanding. Psychological motivations that might have triggered such a response at Pentecost were abundant: the realization that Jesus had been resurrected, an increasing fear of the Jewish authorities, and the inward realization that God's Spirit was present. This kind of "transcendent" communication would solve the difficult problem posed by Luke's use of the term "dialect" (Luke 2:6, 8).

Luke, then, means to say that to the group of Jesus' disciples who were gathered at the festival of Pentecost

[14]C. H. Dodd, *The Apostolic Preaching and Its Development* (New York: Harper, 1937), pp. 57ff.

there came a soul-shaking experience which they — and he — interpreted as the outpouring of the Spirit of God upon them. The external form, however explained, is but a witness to the extraordinary character of the event itself. Moreover, the subsequent behavior of the disciples is sufficient testimony to its lasting effect upon them. This appears to be the central claim of Acts, and this contention is supported in other New Testament books. I Peter, for example, makes this point:

> But rejoice in so far as you share Christ's sufferings, that you may also rejoice and be glad when his glory is revealed. If you are reproached for the name of Christ, you are blessed, because the spirit of glory and of God rests upon you. (I Pet. 4:13-14)

This passage clearly links the messianic community with the Messiah himself. Just as the community shares his sufferings, so it shares his Spirit. A similar thought is found in Hebrews where those who had become partakers of the Messiah are reminded that they are also partakers of the Holy Spirit (see Heb. 3:14 and 6:4). The thought comes to even fuller expression in the writings of Paul. It is a fundamental principle for Paul that through the agency of the Holy Spirit the graces and gifts of the Messiah are reproduced in his people. The Spirit manifested in the Messiah was being further manifested in the members of his body. In effect, Paul drew the Spirit and living Christ closer together, he personalized the Spirit, he ethicized the conception of the Spirit's operation, and he began to present Christianity as the religion of the Spirit. Thus, the general framework of the biblical record is clear. The Spirit is preeminently the title applied to God in action. Before Christ, the Spirit came upon chosen men, inspiring and constraining them to share in divine activity in word and deed. Gradually, a hope emerged of a new age when God's chosen servant — the Messiah — would dwell in men in an altogether unparalleled manner, and when participation in the Spirit would be granted to a far wider community. It is the universal testimony of the New Testament that this day has come in and through Jesus. Especially does Luke set out to indicate step by step the difficulties and obstructions which stand in the way of a truly universal gospel. But in Luke's eyes the outcome is never doubted; God's Spirit will overcome any barrier man constructs.

What, then, is glossolalia in the context of Acts 2? It is the effort to express the inexpressible: the indwelling of the Spirit of God in the lives of men. When the *kerygma* sank home to a responsive heart, ordinary human language could not express the emotions that were aroused; therefore, the believer broke forth in ecstatic speech. These *may* have been intelligible words or phrases, such as "Jesus is Lord" (I Cor. 12:3) or "abba, Father" (Rom. 8:15-16; Gal. 3:6). Other sounds were not recognizable as words at all. At times a continuous, elevated discourse was discernible, perhaps giving the impression that it might be a foreign language. At other times there were inward groanings and sighs too deep for words (Rom. 8:23; 8:26). But it is not legitimate to write off these phenomena as mere gibberish or incoherent nonsense. The speaker was not "out of control." Neither was he in an emotional debauch. Rather, for the believer these manifestations indicated the overwhelming power and presence of the Spirit of God in his life.

In the light of Luke's theological interest — the Spirit of God as power — it is now possible to examine the remaining two references to glossolalia in Acts.

F. Tongues at Caesarea and Ephesus

> While Peter was still saying this, the Holy Spirit fell on all who heard the word. And the believers from among the circumcised who came with Peter were amazed, because the gift of the Holy Spirit had been poured out even on the Gentiles. For they had heard them speaking in tongues and extolling God. (Acts 10:44-46a)

If Philip's mission may be termed a "Samaritan Pentecost," then this incident may well be termed a "Gentile Pentecost."[15] Luke presents Peter as having received

[15]Lindsay Dewar, *The Holy Spirit and Modern Thought* (London: Mowbray, 1959), p. 54.

instructions from the Spirit (Acts 10:19) to go to Cornelius. Peter reluctantly proclaimed to him the good news, and while the apostle was still preaching, the Holy Spirit "fell" on all who heard the word and produced in them the effects of Pentecost, that is, glossolalia. Probably because the case involving Cornelius is unique, Luke dwells upon it at length, relating the account twice (see Acts 11). He is careful to indicate clearly that this gentile convert received the Spirit in exactly the same manner as did the Jewish disciples at Pentecost. It is important to note, then, that the glossolalia occurs in a context where the gospel is breaking through the gentile barrier. Peter earnestly asks, in view of what happened: "Can anyone forbid water for baptizing these people who have received the Holy Spirit just as we have?" (Acts 10:47). Frank Stagg[16] builds a convincing case around this "breaking through" motif, and sees in it the basic theological message of Acts: Luke's writing describes the hard-won liberty of the gospel as it broke down human barriers of separatism and isolation. Luke, then, may well have viewed this instance of glossolalia as another manifestation of the outpouring of the Holy Spirit, paralleling the event of Pentecost.

When Peter returned to Jerusalem he had to relate the entire story of Cornelius point by point in order to clear the air, for there was great conflict in the church about the relationship of the gospel to the gentiles. Was this new religion of Jesus for the gentiles as well as the Jews? The simple fact was that God had come to the house of Cornelius; the Holy Spirit had fallen upon them just as upon the apostles at Pentecost. Glossolalia was an important link in this affirmation, since it had overturned Jewish particularism and opened the church to the gentiles.

Similarly, the incident of glossolalia at Ephesus was Luke's way of indicating that God's approval rested upon the experience of the people there. Ephesus was known as a center of Greek and pagan culture, and Luke saw the gospel's penetration there as but another evidence of the Spirit's shattering of the barrier of Jewish particularism.

[16]Frank Stagg, *The Book of Acts* (Nashville: Broadman, 1955), *passim.*

> And Paul said, "John baptized with the baptism of repentance, telling the people to believe in the one who was to come after him, that is, Jesus." On hearing this, they were baptized in the name of the Lord Jesus. And when Paul had laid his hands upon them, the Holy Spirit came on them; and they spoke with tongues and prophesied. (Acts 19:4-6)

Malcolm Tolbert maintains, with many other scholars, that one of the obvious, primary emphases of Luke-Acts was to demonstrate that the inclusion of "the gentiles in the Christian movement was inherent in the Old Testament, intended by the founder of Christianity, and proceeded under the direction of God."[17] Step by step, then, Luke is intent on showing that it was God — through his Spirit — who impelled men to take the gospel to non-Jews. It was he who validated their efforts by pouring out the Holy Spirit on the new converts who would not have been accepted readily as Christians without some "sign" of God's presence in their lives. The new Samaritan Christians received the Holy Spirit as sign of the genuineness of their conversion. Luke was intent, then, on showing how the various barriers were broken down between Jews, Samaritans, and gentiles. He indicated the presence of God's Spirit at each crossing. In the words of Frank Stagg:

> Pentecost does not stand alone in Acts; it is to be seen along with the giving of the Spirit to others as to Jews: to Samaritans (8:17), in the reaching of the Ethiopian Eunuch, a "God-fearing Greek" (8:29, 39), in the winning of Cornelius, another "God-fearing Gentile" (10:44-47; 11:15), and to former followers of John the Baptist who had not followed Christ (19:6).[18]

Glossolalia in Acts obviously can be understood only through the eyes of the author. In the light of the emphasis placed upon the role of the Spirit in the early Christian community, and in light of Luke's approach to the problem of Jewish isolationism, glossolalia should be seen as *a* legitimate example of the way God worked

[17]Malcolm Tolbert, "Leading Ideas of the Gospel of Luke," *Review and Expositor,* LXIV (Fall 1967), 444.

[18]Frank Stagg, "The Holy Spirit in the New Testament," *Review and Expositor,* LXIII (Spring 1966), 139.

through these Christian pioneers to the end that all men might come into the circle of the redeemed. The phenomenon is an objective manifestation of the power of God's Spirit as it filled these Christians, giving them the requisite power for their mission.

There remains the task of relating these concepts to the Pauline development and reaction to glossolalia, and I want to turn now to I Corinthians.

CHAPTER FOUR

TONGUES IN FIRST CORINTHIANS

I thank God that I speak in tongues more than you all; nevertheless, in church I would rather speak five words with my mind, in order to instruct others, than ten thousand words in a tongue.

I Corinthians 14:18-19

Glossolaliacs and non-glossolaliacs alike have found support for their view in Paul's remarks here. On the one hand, the Pentecostal groups are pleased that Paul can be counted in their number; on the other hand, non-Pentecostals focus on the latter half of the statement and tend to emphasize Paul's disapproval. What factor or set of factors accounts for the apostle's ambivalence here toward glossolalia?

A. The Problem

In I Corinthians 12:1 Paul begins a detailed discussion of spiritual things. This discussion, which stretches through three chapters, is a plea for love, the noblest gift of the Spirit. This gift has as its goal rational preaching that is in sharp contrast to the glossolalia which is causing dissension and individualism at Corinth. The contents of these chapters reveal that Paul had a deeper knowledge of the problem of glossolalia at Corinth. He devotes Chapter 14 to an examination of glossolalia and its interpretation and to prophecy.

Paul begins his discussion of spiritual gifts by differentiating between Christian experience and pagan worship, no matter how real (I Cor. 12:1-3). The pagan gods are idols or demons who must be carefully distinguished from the Spirit of God (I Cor. 12:1). Paul specifically mentions, as a *charisma,* the gift of distinguishing between spirits (I Cor. 12:10). It is reasonable to assume that in Paul's mind the gift of discernment would enable one to determine whether glossolalia was spoken by the Spirit of God or was demonic in origin.

Paul lists some of the spiritual gifts twice. Included within these lists are the discernment of spirits, prophecy, kinds of tongues, and the interpretation of tongues (I Cor. 12:8-10; 12:28-30). Although his whole argument is to emphasize that no one gift is superior to another in the body of Christ, it is interesting that in both instances he places "kinds of tongues" and "interpretation of tongues" last. In Chapter 13, on the other hand, the gift of tongues comes first on the list, but here the gifts seem to be enumerated in an order of increasing value.

Of these three chapters dealing with spiritual gifts, it is Chapter 14 that contains the discussion of glossolalia. Inevitably the sense of the Greek is obscured in English translation. The King James Version, for example, added the word "unknown," thereby conveying an idea somewhat foreign to the text. The Goodspeed translation renders "speaking in tongues" with the phrase "speak ecstatically." Obviously a special English word is needed, and some translators use "glossolalia."

Finally, it is helpful to bear in mind that Paul does not present a thorough, descriptive analysis of the nature and value of glossolalia; on the contrary, he is intent to deal pastorally with the problem in Corinth since the "spiritual ones" have overemphasized glossolalia to the neglect of prophecy in the vernacular.

B. Interpreting Paul on Glossolalia

Scholars have taken three basic approaches to understanding what Paul says about glossolalia in I Corinthians.

In each case, tongue-speaking is seen to have grown out of a different background.

1. The Hellenistic Background of Glossolalia

Varied cultures, races, religions, and philosophies mingled at Corinth. There was a multiplicity of temples and religious statues in the city. Since the Christians in Corinth were converts from Judaism and paganism, the background of rivalry was potentially dangerous to the Corinthian church. Therefore, some scholars assume that Paul's discussion of tongues was in answer to the question: By what criterion can divine and demonic ecstasy be distinguished from each other? Quite possibly the debate in Corinth over spiritual gifts, especially tongues, had built up to a point where serious division threatened the fellowship, the worship, and above all, the missionary enterprise.

The assumption that glossolalia at Corinth was similar to the ecstatic utterances of the Hellenistic religions is accepted by many notable scholars.[1] To establish this relation, scholars point to the examples of ecstaticism in Hellenistic religion.

The most famous of all the ecstatic prophets of Greece was the Pythia at Delphi, who is Plato's first example of prophetic madness in the *Phaedras*. The god would enter into her vocal organs and use them as if they were his own. He spoke through her in the first person, not the third. Even before the inquirer would enter the temple, the Pythia was under the influence of the god and was in some abnormal state of trance or ecstasy. The chief priest would ask the inquirer's question. The answer would vary in coherence and intelligibility. When it had been given, the chief priest would dictate it to the inquirer.

Since it is impossible to know the exact nature of the speech of the Pythia, an examination of the nature of her

[1]See, for example, Jean Héring, *The First Epistle of Saint Paul to the Corinthians,* trans. A. W. Heathcote and P. J. Allcock (London: Epworth, 1962), p. 128; Elias Andrews, "Tongues, Gift of," *The Interpreter's Dictionary of the Bible,* ed. George Arthur Buttrick, 4 vols. (Nashville: Abingdon, 1962), R-Z, 671; James Moffatt, *The First Epistle of Paul to the Corinthians* (New York: Harper, 1933), pp. 207-208.

inspiration is the only course open in seeking to understand her relationship to glossolalia. The most reliable description of the psychological state of the Pythia comes from Plutarch, who possibly received the information first-hand from the prophet Nicander. While the incident he relates was certainly an exceptional occurrence, it does reveal some important features of the ecstatic prophetesses at Delphi.

> When, then, the imaginative and prophetic faculty is in a state of proper adjustment for attempering itself to the spirit as to a drug, inspiration in those who foretell the future is bound to come; and whenever the conditions are not thus, it is bound not to come, or when it does come to be misleading, abnormal and confusing, as we know in the case of the priestess who died not so long ago. As it happened, a deputation from abroad had arrived to consult the oracle. The victim (*i.e.*, the goat to be sacrificed), it is said, remained unmoved and unaffected in any way by the first libations; but the priests, in their eagerness to please, went far beyond their wonted usage, and only after the victim had been subjected to a deluge and nearly drowned did it at last give in (*i.e.*, shiver). What then, was the result touching the priestess? She went down into the oracle unwillingly, they say, and half-heartedly; and at her first responses it was at once plain from the harshness of her voice that she was not responding properly; she was like a labouring ship and was filled with a mighty and baleful spirit. Finally she became hysterical and with a frightful shriek rushed towards the exit and threw herself down, with the result that not only the members of the deputation fled but also the oracle interpreter Nicander and those holy men that were present. However, after a little, they went in and took her up, still conscious; and she lived on for a few days.[2]

This account indicates that the trance or ecstasy was still genuine in Plutarch's time. This change in voice is mentioned elsewhere in Plutarch as a common feature of "enthusiasm." Though definite evidence is lacking, it appears that the Pythia's inspiration was due to "possession." Further, it is interesting to note that while the oracles were like the mysteries in using a physical means to induce the

---

[2]Plutarch, *The Obsolescence of Oracles*, 438, 51, in *Plutarch's Moralia*, trans. Frank Cole Babbit, 10 vols., The Loeb Classical Library (London: Heinemann, 1944-1949), V, 499.

state of inspiration, they differed substantially in the purpose and result of their efforts. The purpose of the oracles was evidently to gain some *knowledge* from the god; the mysteries sought to achieve *union* with the god, a union that resulted in frenzied confusion.

The Sibyl also belonged to the group of ecstatic prophetesses of the pagan world, and therefore some scholars allege that she manifested glossolalia. The first mention of the Sibyl is in Heraclitus. He notes that "the Sibyl with raving voice speaks words that have no part in laughter or in rich apparel or in unguents. Yet she prevails; for it is the god who drives her."[3] Her oracles were composed in verse. Cicero noted that they were frequently composed with an acrostic — the first letter of each verse taken in order conveyed a meaning. Just as at Delphi, interpreters were needed; thus the original speech may have been unintelligible.

a. Similarities. First, it is apparent that the Pythia at Delphi demonstrated divine madness or ecstasy. The reaction of the spectators was similar to that reflected in the Corinthian letter when Paul indicates that outsiders might consider the participants mad (Acts 2:13b). Second, disorder and confusion seem to have been evident in both the Corinthian worship and among the pagan rites cited above. Finally, the use of intoxication in the Bacchic revelries parallels the criticism of some of the onlookers at Pentecost that "they [the disciples] are filled with new wine" (Acts 16:16. Cf. Eph. 5:18).

b. Differences. The significance of the ecstatic state was different for Paul than for the mysteries, Plato, and the oracles. In these latter instances, the emphasis was upon learning the secrets of the gods; in the former the end was meaningful communion (but not union) with God who had bestowed this gift of the Holy Spirit. Also, it is significant that Paul consistently maintained a distinction between tongues and prophecy, a distinction which did not exist in the other pagan rites.

[3] Fragment 92 in Hermann Diels, *Die Fragmente der Vorsokratiker,* 2 vols. (Berlin: Weidmann, 1951-1952), I, iii, 94.

In Paul's exhortation to the Ephesians, "Do not get drunk with wine, for this is debauchery, but be filled with the Spirit" (Eph. 5:18), the relationship of inebriation and inspiration to that of the intoxication in the Bacchic reveries is that of opposition and not agreement, showing only outward similarity. In the Bacchic rites, the ecstatic experience was sought after per se, and furthermore was induced by artificial means. The New Testament does not betray such artificiality. The infilling of the Holy Spirit comes without psychological inducements. The Spirit-filled person remains in full control of his gifts (I Cor. 14:32-33; 14:39-40). Again, the oracles were consulted for information known only to the gods, and the prophetess did not speak voluntarily. Those who interpreted these oracles took the initiative in posing the questions to the oracle, and often their "interpretation" was as vague as the oracle itself. In Paul, it is Christ who approaches the believer.

In the Hellenistic religions, there appears to be a loss of self-control in the ecstatic state. Paul, however, presupposes that the believers at Corinth should control the gift of tongues. In fact, he offers certain specific suggestions to aid in achieving a degree of orderliness.

Finally, the ethical implications mark the most apparent difference. In paganism there is no parallel to the teaching of Paul in I Corinthians that the Spirit ministers love within the congregation. Paul definitely attributed ethical conduct to the work of the Spirit (Rom. 8:4-9).

c. Conclusion. While there likely is a certain formal, external connection between the ecstaticism of certain pagan religious practices and glossolalia, the phenomenon about which Paul wrote in I Corinthians 14, when rightly understood and practiced, does not signify concepts identical to those for which certain ecstatic phenomena stood. It is fallacious to argue that because of certain parallelisms, Corinthian glossolalia at its deepest level betrayed the same meaning as the ecstatic frenzies of the Hellenistic religions. That its *form* bore some semblance to these phenomena is most probable, however.

2. The Background of Glossolalia in the Psyche of Mankind

Although glossolalia appears to be a religious phenomenon, it can be studied from a socio-psychological viewpoint. Much is to be learned concerning the phenomenon from a psychological perspective, and some scholars see the origin of glossolalia not as peculiar to Corinth — or to biblical history — but as representative of the psychological constituent of mankind, which is a factor present in every age.

a. Glossolalia as a psychopathic phenomenon. Since William James suggested that a psychopathic temperament was often present in religious leaders, students of psychology of religion have not hesitated to consider the possibility of psychopathic involvement in religious experience.

The most comprehensive book in the English-speaking world dealing with glossolalia from a psychological point of view is George B. Cutten's *Speaking with Tongues: Historically and Psychologically Considered,* which describes the phenomenon as something that can be "explained by recognized psychological laws."[4] Cutten classifies glossolalia as a religious experience having symptoms similar to allied phenomena like hysteria and catalepsy. He shows, for example, that the hysteric, like the glossolaliac, is most susceptible to suggestion and manifests exaggerated sensations and weird bodily contortions during his periods of rapture. On the other hand, it is important to note that while hysteria was once a common occurrence, especially among women, genuine cases of hysteria in recent years have been increasingly difficult to isolate. Also, it is significant that, judging from the extant materials from the apostolic period, glossolalia was predominantly a phenomenon among men rather than women, whereas Cutten observes that "in all forms of nervous instability females predominate, and in hysteria they are in the proportion of

---

[4]George B. Cutten, *Speaking with Tongues: Historically and Psychologically Considered* (New Haven: Yale University, 1927), p. 181.

twenty females to one male."[5] In the light of this fact, it is interesting that in the modern tongues movement, women are more numerous.

b. Glossolalia as ecstaticism and related phenomena. It is much more common in psychological circles to explain glossolalia as a manifestation of ecstasy in which verbal automatisms are expressed from the unconscious. Emile Lombard notes that

> in terms more directly borrowed from the vocabulary of modern psychology, we are concerned with a state of personal disaggregation, in which the speech-motor center of the subject obeys subconscious impulses. The glossolalia is an *automatic* phenomenon, which signifies only that it be loosed of all voluntary and cognate character; *automatic* means here, foreign to the conscious "Ego," being a modality and a part of the total "I."[6]

Eddison Mosiman has compared glossolalia to a state of hypnosis. He points to the parallels between the conditions used to produce a hypnotic state and those exhibited by the glossolaliac: fixation of attention, uniformity of perception, limitation of the power of the will, and suppression of ideas. Aside from terminology, Mosiman appears to agree with Lombard. He observes that

> the essence of the psychological explanation of speaking with tongues is an utterance of thought and feeling through the speech organ, which temporarily is under the control of the reflexive nerve center, and the special forms are primarily attributed to the suggestion which mainly arises out of a literal understanding of the New Testament.[7]

Ira J. Martin, who has written extensively on the subject of glossolalia, concedes that "glossolalia appears to be an ecstatic form of speech, seeking to give vent to the joy of the new life of spiritual redemption."[8] He contends, how-

[5]*Ibid.*, p. 159.

[6]Emile Lombard, *De la Glossolalie chez les premiers chrétiens et des phénomènes similaires* (Lausanne: Bridel, 1910), p. 6.

[7]Eddison Mosiman, *Das Zungenreden geschichtlich und psychologisch untersucht* (Tübingen: Mohr, 1911), p. 114.

[8]Ira J. Martin, *Glossolalia in the Apostolic Church: A Survey Study of Tongue-Speech* (Berea, Kentucky: Berea College, 1960), p. 100.

ever, that glossolalia is one form of psychic catharsis, "a genuine but not universal concomitant of the Christian conversion experience." Furthermore, Martin differentiates two types of glossolalia: the genuine and the synthetic. The former represents a "psychic catharsis," while the latter occurs when other factors are operating — for example, auto-hypnosis, normal hypnosis, the laws of auto-suggestion.[9]

Lombard suggests a three-fold classification of "automatic speech." These "types" represent degrees of progression from the remote forms to the nearer and more familiar forms of organized language. First, there are inarticulate sounds such as hiccups, cries, sighs, wailings, and murmurs. These simple vocal sounds are especially apparent in glossolaliacs at the beginning of their automatism. The second classification encompasses the most common type of glossolalia, a pseudo-language or speech composed of articulate sounds resembling words. There is actually a phonic differentiation, and the person *seems* to be speaking and expressing definite ideas. In reality, however, the language itself is meaningless and has no content. Finally, there are "manufactured" or "coined" words (neologisms) which emerge upon a base of well-characterized pseudo-language and have a constant representative value or meaning.

c. Glossolalia as unconscious memory. The previous discussions have viewed glossolalia as a meaningless language. A third approach regards the glossolalia as real foreign languages uttered from the unconscious memory of an individual, which is not consciously known or understood. The memory is apparently capable of storing away all of the impressions that enter consciousness. William Cullen Bryant in old age said that if he were given a few moments for reflection he could recite any line he had ever written. Memory deposits that have supposedly been long forgotten, or even so fully forgotten that there is no memory

___

[9]Andrew D. Lester, "Glossolalia: A Psychological Evaluation" (unpublished seminar paper, Southern Baptist Theological Seminary, Louisville, Kentucky, 1965), p. 10.

that they ever existed at all, have been recalled. Evidently Arthur Wright was the first in the period of modern psychology to offer this explanation of glossolalia.[10] Both Jerusalem and Corinth were cosmopolitan areas — as were Ephesus and Caesarea — and the glossolalia could have been words and phrases of many different languages stored unconsciously in the memory of the speakers until released at a time of ecstatic rapture.

There is little question from a psychological perspective that this explanation is possible. There are too many clinical examples of an unlearned foreign language in the personal unconscious to deny flatly the existence of such phenomena. There remains, however, for the biblical theologian, regardless of whether this is actually what happened at Corinth and Jerusalem, the task of determining *meaning.* It is difficult to understand Paul's position with respect to glossolalia if in fact it were simply a foreign language; and it is even more difficult to account for its rather dramatic effect at Pentecost if it were only repressed foreign language. The clinical examples of this phenomenon today are not nearly so dramatic or impressive. Such a view undercuts the significance of glossolalia as a *charisma,* and voids the Pauline concept of the "gift of interpretation."

Thus, while the psychological approach is helpful and descriptive, one must search elsewhere to discover the origin of glossolalia at Corinth.

3. *The Palestinian Background of Glossolalia*

A third group of scholars holds that the primary background for the Corinthian glossolalia was Hebraic and not Hellenistic, though there was obviously some modification of the phenomenon at Corinth. Philo, for example, enumerates four types of ecstasy: (1) mad fury producing mental delusion; (2) extreme amazement; (3) mental tran-

[10]Arthur Wright, *Some New Testament Problems* (London: Methuen, 1898), pp. 277-303.

quillity of vacancy; (4) divine possession or frenzy of the prophets.[11] He may have had Plato's *Phaedras* in mind, since he employs the term *mania*. He describes the ecstatic prophet as having "no utterance of his own, but all his utterances came from elsewhere, the echoes of another's voice. . . ."[12] Elsewhere Philo writes:

> Nothing of what he says will be his own, for he that is truly under the control of divine inspiration has no power of apprehension when he speaks as the channel for the insistent words of another's prompting.[13]

Again, he states that divination is a corruption or a counterfeit of divine and prophetic possession. It becomes clear, then, that Philo's concept of ecstatic prophecy was that of divine possession in which all conscious control by the prophet was abdicated to the divine Spirit. While there is no indication that these references describe a phenomenon parallel to the Corinthian glossolalia, they do furnish a background which would tolerate such expressions of possession by the Spirit.

The closest Philo comes to describing what occurred at Corinth is his description of the Hebrew name "Hannah," which means "grace."

> When grace fills the soul, that soul thereby rejoices and smiles and dances, for it is possessed and inspired, so that to many of the unenlightened it may seem to be drunken, crazy and beside itself. . . . For with the God-possessed not only is the soul wont to be stirred and goaded as it were into ecstasy but the body also is flushed and fiery, warmed by the overflowing joy within which passes on the sensation to the outer man, and thus many of the foolish are deceived and suppose that the sober are drunk.[14]

Maurice Barnett suggests the impossibility of a pagan cult having given rise to glossolalia at Corinth because Paul speaks of the attendant problems as though they were quite unfamiliar to the Corinthian Christians. In Barnett's

[11] Philo, *Who Is the Heir,* 249, in *Philo,* trans. Ralph Marcus, 10 vols., The Loeb Classical Library (London: Heinemann, 1939-1953), IV, 409-411.

[12] *Ibid.,* 417.

[13] Philo, *On the Special Law Books,* I, 65, in Marcus, VII, 137.

[14] Philo, *On Drunkenness,* XXXVI, 146-147, in Marcus, III, 395.

view, this indicates that these Christians were in fact in need of instruction and guidance.[15] Following a suggestion made by T. W. Manson, Barnett theorizes that the Cephas party was seeking to impose upon the Christian community there the same type of ecstatic frenzy which had characterized the original outpouring of the Spirit at Pentecost. In keeping with their Judaistic ritual emphasis, the Cephas party was more interested in the external form than the essential meaning of the phenomenon. It was the requirement of this party that all Corinthian Christians who received the Spirit show the same external signs of its presence.

While it is not certain that the Cephas party was the Judaizing influence, as Barnett claims, his point about the Corinthian problem's being bound up with pagan excesses is relevant. He notes that in every pagan rite ecstatic experiences were sought and that artificial means were often used to induce a state of uncontrollable excitement, which became false ecstasy. But in the New Testament there is no artificiality; ecstasy comes first and the strange utterances are the outward sign of this inward condition. The Spirit comes upon persons and *then* they speak with other tongues. Quite possibly it was the *artificiality* with which Paul was dealing in the Corinthian letter. Perhaps the pagan practices in Corinth served only to confuse a stimulated ecstasy with the characteristic Hebraic spirit possession that came suddenly and unexpectedly upon a person. There may have been at Corinth the same problem of distinguishing between ecstasy and true spirit possession as existed in Israel when prophetism came into contact with the bands of Canaanite prophets.

Paul could not tolerate a type of ecstasy that isolated the individual from normal social relations with his fellow worshippers. As W. D. Davies notes:

> Paul's conception of the Spirit in the light of Rabbinic Judaism . . . has one aspect which sets it wholly apart from what we found in Hellenism, namely its communal character.[16]

[15]Maurice Barnett, *The Living Flame* (London: Epworth, 1953), p. 106.
[16]W. D. Davies, *Paul and Rabbinic Judaism* (London: S.P.C.K., 1948), p. 200.

Paul acknowledges the divine origin of glossolalia (I Cor. 14:2), but he also reminds the Corinthians not to be excessive in their practice of the gift (I Cor. 14:27). He is seeking a proper balance within the church life between the sensational aspects of the Spirit and the more sedate and beneficial aspects of its endowment.

The issue is simply that the *charismata* were sometimes made ends in themselves and eagerly sought for as signs of superiority over other Christians. While certain individuals were eager for manifestations of the presence of the Spirit, they did not use these manifestations to build up the church (I Cor. 14:12). Rather, those who excelled in extraordinary gifts, particularly glossolalia, paraded them (I Cor. 13:4-5); they looked down upon less gifted Christians (I Cor. 12:21); they often caused intolerable confusion in the worship services (I Cor. 14:33). Obviously, the seeking of *charismata* for their own sake led to the counterfeiting of them (see I Cor. 12:3). Thus, the gift of distinguishing the true from the false manifestations became necessary (I Cor. 12:10). By the end of the New Testament era, the problem had become acute:

> Beloved, do not believe every spirit, but test the spirits to see whether they are of God; for many false prophets have gone out into the world. By this you know the Spirit of God: every spirit which confesses that Jesus Christ has come in the flesh is of God, and every spirit which does not confess Jesus is not of God. By this we know the spirit of truth and the spirit of error. (I John 4:1-3a; 4:6b)

It is here suggested that the *charismata* and related phenomena are properly understood as a part of the Spirit's witness to the *kerygma*. Hence the proper starting point is not I Corinthians 12-14, where there is a situation in which these *charismata* are being overemphasized, but rather, the passages where the *kerygma* is being preached and the Spirit bears witness to its validity. Thus approached, the *charismata* remain extraordinary and superhuman, but not nonsensical or bizarre. They form a coherent picture not of human autosuggestion and mass excitement, but of the working of the Spirit whose power invades human life to bear witness to the truth of the *kerygma.*

Paul's main objection is not to the practice of glossolalia so much as to the *estimate* of the practice. In I Corinthians 12:1-3 he asserts that all Christians are "spiritual ones" by virtue of their baptismal confession (I Cor. 12:13). The entire twelfth chapter makes the basic point that there is diversity and equal authenticity among the various gifts of the Spirit. It appears that pneumatic status was being denied at Corinth to those who could not produce the more sensational signs like glossolalia and claimed exclusively for those who did. That is to say, there is evidently the claim that tongues serve as a "sign" for the Christians. It would be a simple step from tongues as *a* sign to tongues as *the* sign.

> The one and only reason which Paul gives for allowing the use of tongues in the presence of others is that they may serve to attract the attention of unbelievers, and even this seems to be curiously at variance with the later comment that "outsiders" coming in will think people who talk in tongues are mad — unless verse 22 refers to one single person talking in tongues and verse 23 to the confusion when several speak together.[17]

It is important, then, to distinguish glossolalia from the *problem* of glossolalia. As J. P. M. Sweet concludes: "The problem . . . was new, and lay not in a surfeit of, but in a demand for, glossolalia. . . ."[18] If Paul were not attacking tongues per se, but rather the estimate of their value, then his positive statements can be allowed to speak for themselves. Evidence outside the epistle itself indicates that Paul's attitude was reserved but not altogether negative: Paul recognizes tongues as a *charisma,* but his concept of *charismata* is substantially different from that of the Corinthians. To them the *charismata* were something extraordinary and supernatural. To Paul, however, they were something more. Specifically, the *charismata* are the expression of the church's ministry (see I Cor. 12).

[17]"Notes on Recent Exposition," *Expository Times,* LXXVIII (May, 1966), 227.

[18]J. P. M. Sweet, "A Sign for Unbelievers: Paul's Attitude to Glossolalia," *New Testament Studies,* XIII (April, 1967), 249.

In the light of the foregoing discussion, what conclusions may be drawn from Paul's discussion of glossolalia? The following are suggested: (1) Paul rejects the claim that tongues are the only (I Cor. 12:30) or even the normal sign of the presence of the Spirit of God. (2) His condemnation of glossolalia is not absolute, but made in relation to other *charismata* (I Cor. 12:6-10; 12:28-30). While he valued it highly as a private experience (I Cor. 14:4; cf. I Cor. 14:18-19), the fact that it was private meant that it could not "build up," and therefore he regarded it as inferior to those activities that could (I Cor. 14:3). (3) Paul does not regard glossolalia as childish; rather it is the Corinthians' estimate of it that he considers childish. He was anxious that the Corinthian Christians not allow their idea of the spiritual to be narrowed to a point where it would be dominated by the least valuable gift (I Cor. 12:6-10; 12:28-30; 14:3). (4) In light of the conspicuous absence of any reference to tongues in Romans 12, it is all but impossible to claim Pauline authority for regarding glossolalia as a necessary part of the Christian life. On the other hand, it is obviously fallacious to claim that Paul held it to be devil-inspired and completely without value.

Paul's ambivalence, then, can be explained partially by the danger of allowing tongues to become the sole sign of the presence of God's Spirit. But the relationship of Acts to I Corinthians on the matter of glossolalia suggests that there may well have been an additional reason.

C. The Relationship of Acts and First Corinthians

Elias Andrews has stated that "plainly an irreconcilable difference exists between the Lukan account in Acts 2:4 and Pauline accounts."[19] Such a statement is justification for the importance of this section of the investigation.

Earlier it was suggested that Luke added the foreign-language motif to the account in Acts 2. There are several possible motivations, and Luke's redaction may have been the result of any one or a combination of these factors.

[19] Andrews, p. 671.

1. Jewish Parallels

a. The theophany at Mount Sinai. Some scholars note that Luke seems to have had in the background of his thought the giving of the law at Sinai. Could it be that Luke describes the phenomenon the way he does, not because he misunderstood glossolalia, but because he wanted to emphasize the parallels to the theophany at Sinai? There can be little doubt that the giving of the law is in the background of Luke's thought. The wind, the tongues of fire, and even the glossolalia itself, all resemble the manifestations of the Spirit of God at Sinai. Furthermore, the contrast of the age of the law and the new age of the Spirit is self-evident. The Jews taught that the law was given so that it was understood in all languages:

> Although the ten commandments were promulgated with a single sound, it says, "all people heard the voices"; it follows then that when the voice went forth it was divided into seven voices, and then went into seventy tongues, and every people received the law in their own language.[20]

b. The Tower of Babel. Another Old Testament parallel which has fascinated scholars is the story of the Tower of Babel. The obvious contrast between the Babel story and the Pentecostal experience may well have been in Luke's mind when he wrote his narrative. In the beginning, according to Philo, man had only one language that was intelligible to all humans. The confusion of men's languages occurred at the building of the Tower of Babel. Evidently, there was the expectation that at some time in the future the people of the Lord would again have one language.[21] The idea is that Luke has utilized the Old Testament version of the Tower of Babel as a model. Whereas in the Old Testament account the languages were confused, in Acts 2 they are ordered again, and each one hears in his own language.

A linguistic comparison does indicate that Luke de-

---

[20]Midrash Tanhuma quoted in Dale Moody, *Spirit of the Living God* (Philadelphia: Westminster, 1968), p. 72.

[21]See Judah 25:3, *Testament of the XII Patriarchs.*

pended upon the Genesis story for some of his vocabulary; however, little more can be safely claimed.

2. *Pauline Influence*

Another theory which might account for Luke's shaping of the primitive account so as to include the foreign-language motif is tied to Luke's relationship with Paul. It is suggested that Luke, under Pauline influence, sought to reinterpret the original speaking in tongues so as to avoid the Pauline criticism of disorder and unintelligibility. The theory that Luke and Paul were in fact traveling companions has given credence to this position. Furthermore, the acquaintance of the two men could explain not only the alteration in the Lukan narrative, but also, in some measure, Paul's ambivalence on the subject of glossolalia. If Luke did avail himself of sources, however disputed and undefined, it is reasonable to assume that the Corinthian Christians also heard of this Jerusalem "tradition." Paul's respect for Luke, as well as the close association of the events of Pentecost with the apostles, among whom he sought diligently to be numbered himself, could in some small way help explain his refusal to condemn the phenomenon per se, despite the serious reservations he had when he learned of the excesses at Corinth.

3. *Psychological Communication*

Again, Luke may have taken the view that the communication which transpired at Pentecost was not a kind of speech that would be intelligible to a disinterested spectator, but that within the context of the community it was nevertheless a form of language which, under the right conditions and by the right people, could be understood. Wayne Oates points out that there was a "subsoil" of devoutness among those who "heard." The Holy Spirit energized this kind of communication among those who were a part of this community. Oates concludes that this type of communication is

> highly communal — those who understand each other eat to-

gether in gladness and singleness of heart. This understanding is reciprocal — no one person is left to do all the understanding in one-way communication.[22]

While this sort of community may well have existed in Jerusalem at Pentecost, it is most unlikely that it existed in even the remotest form at Corinth. In fact, I Corinthians seems to indicate that it did not. From the questions to which Paul addressed himself in that epistle it appears that the Corinthian church was problem-ridden. There was division among the membership there (I Cor. 1:10ff.). A certain individual was evidently living with his father's wife, and the church apparently was indifferent to the situation (I Cor. 5:1-13). Church members were suing one another in pagan courts of law (I Cor. 6:1-11). Some of the Christians were turning grace into license, and Paul had to remind them that members of the body of Christ must not give their own bodies to harlots (I Cor. 6:15). Others boasted over their knowledge (I Cor. 8), while still others selfishly employed freedom to the hurt of others in the name of personal "rights" (I Cor. 9). The services of worship were disorderly (I Cor. 11:1-6), and some turned the Lord's Supper into a private supper club with clannish indulgences (I Cor. 11:17-34). Certainly Corinth, then, was lacking as a community where psychological communication might take place.

Any or all of these reasons might account for Luke's particular slant in his presentation of the material in the Pentecost narrative. My main contention is that I Corinthians deals with a particular historical situation where the concept of the Spirit of God as power is absent. The result is division and disunity.

D. Conclusion

The following statements are suggested in light of the preceding discussion.

(1) Tongues are obviously alluded to, and specifically mentioned in I Corinthians.

(2) Paul is ambivalent in his attitude, that is, he con-

---

[22]Wayne E. Oates, "The Holy Spirit and the Overseer of the Flock," *Review and Expositor,* LXIII (Spring 1966), 188.

fesses that he speaks with tongues "more than you all," and yet he calls for certain restrictions in the practice of glossolalia among the Corinthian Christians. The former position is the natural outgrowth of (a) his association with Luke; (b) his knowledge of the Pentecost tradition; (c) his desire to demonstrate his apostleship. The latter position stems from his conviction that there was a vast difference between Corinthian and Pentecostal glossolalia. He realizes that (a) in the light of the Greek ecstatic background, the Corinthian glossolalia may be only an imitation of the Pentecostal concept of possession by the Spirit; (b) there is an excessive demand for glossolalia to be *the* sign of spirit possession; (c) there ought to be order in worship and church life; (d) all spiritual gifts ought to build up the church and issue in service.

(3) Finally, Paul's *basic* theory of the validity of tongues is not at variance with Luke's. The difference lies rather in the significance attached to the phenomenon. In keeping with the concept of the Spirit of God which manifests itself through the several gifts of the Spirit and in light of the particular historical setting in which the church at Corinth found itself, it appears that to interpret glossolalia biblically for the church today, the Lukan material should be considered primary.

CHAPTER FIVE

RECONSTRUCTION AND REAPPRAISAL

God is trying to get through into the Church, staid and stuffy and self-centered as it often is, with a kind of power that will make it radiant and exciting and self-giving. We should seek to understand and be reverent toward this phenomenon, rather than to ignore or scorn it.

Samuel M. Shoemaker

Much of the disagreement concerning glossolalia today would subside if there could be a distinction drawn between the meaning of the form and the symbolism of the phenomenon. Many non-Pentecostal scholars who totally reject speaking in tongues would not hesitate to insist that the Holy Spirit can play a meaningful role in the lives of contemporary Christians. Similarly, by focusing upon the totality of the phenomena which attest to the Spirit's presence, and by viewing glossolalia as only one of these, some Pentecostals who possess the gift of tongue-speech might refrain from regarding their gift as superior to all others. A contemporary Christian with a modern, twentieth-century world hypothesis might "stumble" at the *form* of glossolalia as it is presented in the New Testament, but this same Christian might well concede that this outmoded structure once represented the power and presence of God to the early Christians. While he would not accept the form, he might well share a similar belief about the availability of God's power and presence in the world today. As Lester Cleveland observes:

> When glossolalia first appeared in Christian circles, men of other religious persuasions commonly accepted it as the mark of possession by the gods. It undoubtedly made a profound impression on these people and a strong witness for Christianity.
>
> Our world view is so different today most people look upon it as a sign of insanity or fanaticism, if not both. Love is hardly increased by these reactions.[1]

But having said this, Cleveland cautions that we must still recognize the value in a demythologized glossolalia. That is, somehow there must be a way to strip tongue-speech of its repulsive outer appearance and see it beneath its veneer. To put it another way, is it possible for the nonparticipating Christian to "get inside" his glossolaliac brother and see first hand what's going on? How does the world look? The church? If the movement is to be understood, it seems that we must first listen to *him* — not to his often loud and random speech sounds, but to him. We must listen to him in order to discover what all this "noise" really signifies.

Thus in attempting to survey the overall relevance of glossolalia for the church today, we will explore both the formal and the symbolic avenues of meaning.

A. The Formal Structure of Glossolalia

1. The Reality of Glossolalia

That glossolalia occurred among the early Christians cannot be denied. Further, instances of the phenomenon can be documented outside Christendom, as well as in the history of the Christian church. Obviously, while apparent in the first century, glossolalia was not unique to that age. Yet, it appears that neither the Pentecostal event itself

---

[1] Lester D. Cleveland, "Let's Demythologize Glossolalia," *The Baptist Program*, XLV (June, 1967), 11.

nor any of the subsequent manifestations of the phenomenon has had any significant apologetic thrust among the nonparticipants. At Pentecost at least part of the crowd scoffed at this manifestation of the Spirit, linking it with the "babbling" of drunkards. Luke represents Peter as the one who shrewdly proceeded to defend the actions of the disciples who uttered these strange sounds. Peter evidently spoke in his ordinary tongue, and, judging from the results of his preaching, was highly effective (Acts 2:41).

At Corinth the *charismata* were made ends in themselves and were sought after as signs of superiority to be used superciliously over other Christians. The Christians there were "eager for manifestations of the Spirit," but apparently did not use them to build up the church (I Cor. 14:12). Those who excelled in extraordinary gifts, particularly glossolalia, paraded them (I Cor. 12:4-5) and looked down upon the less gifted Christians (I Cor. 12:21); they also produced intolerable confusion in the services of worship (I Cor. 14:33). In time, those who sought the various *charismata* for their own sake began to counterfeit these gifts. Thus, the gift of distinguishing the true from the false was necessary within the context of the church. At the close of the first century, the problem had become acute:

> Beloved, do not believe every spirit, but test the spirits to see whether they are of God; for many false prophets have gone out into the world. By this you know the Spirit of God: every spirit which confesses that Jesus Christ has come in the flesh is of God. (I John 4:1-2)

Thus, the writer of I John indicates that the Christian could no longer trust what appeared to be the working of the Spirit. Rather, he had to carefully examine "every spirit."

a. Values. While Paul saw no value in glossolalia for the church as a whole (I Cor. 14:2; 14:4; 14:5; 14:19; 14:28), he evidently recognized some personal reward for the individual who spoke in tongues. Also, Paul realized that glossolalia could potentially serve as a sign to convince an unbeliever that God existed and exerted his power upon men. Perhaps Paul best expresses his estimate of glossolalia when he writes: ". . . in church I would rather speak five words with my mind, in order to instruct others, than ten thousand words in a tongue" (I Cor. 14:19). Thus, while Paul did not deny that glossolalia was a valid *charisma,* he did deny that it was to be exalted to first place as the sole evidence of the indwelling of God's Spirit. In fact, the apostle noted that it was inferior to prophecy (I Cor. 14:5), and in his list of gifts in I Corinthians 12, tongue-speaking comes last. Yet Paul was unwilling to write off the phenomenon completely, indicating that it could be a meaningful part of the worship service provided certain regulations were adhered to: (1) there should not be more than three glossolaliacs speaking during a single service (I Cor. 14:27); (2) of those allowed to speak, only one should speak at a time (I Cor. 14:27); (3) and this one should speak only when someone who can interpret is present, either the glossolaliac himself or someone else (I Cor. 14:27).

Luke, on the other hand, does not assess the value of the gift per se; however, his writings presuppose belief in a God whose Spirit is active in the proclamation of the gospel — a God who vindicates the work of the apostles by demonstrating through some sign his presence and power.

b. Dangers. According to Paul's own teaching (Gal. 5:16-26), a demonstration of the indwelling of the Spirit was requisite to the Christian life; however, because glossolalia had become the standard whereby all charismatic gifts were to be judged, Paul advocated strict controls for its use. Glossolalia demonstrated the presence of the Spirit as an external sign which of itself had no value. But at Corinth this sign had degenerated into the sensational, the showy, the gaudy. The Corinthian Christians appeared to have overlooked the fact that a demonstration of the Spirit's presence ought to reflect to some degree the character of that Spirit itself. Indeed, Paul emphasized this when he developed love as the greatest of all the *charismata* (I Cor. 13:13).

2. A Critical Evaluation of the Form Structure of Glossolalia

It is understandable that the Christians of the first century chose glossolalia as the proof that the Holy Spirit had come upon them. The early church was born and grew in a hostile environment, and a clear, outward sign of the Spirit's presence was necessary to indicate to the unbelievers that the work of the gospel was legitimate.

Today, for the mainstream of Protestantism, public instances of glossolalia bring confusion, disunity, and disillusionment. From the perspective of many non-Pentecostals, glossolalia is a weird, esoteric phenomenon that belongs to immature Christians who come from a low socio-economic background and who possess a fundamentalist understanding of life and the faith. On the other hand, viewed through the eyes of their Pentecostal brothers, these same "mainstream" Protestants lack the "baptism of the Spirit." While the non-Pentecostals point to the whole context of glossolalia as a "highly charged atmosphere," the glossolaliacs note that the phenomenon "can also occur in quiet surroundings, and the unleashing of emotionalism is simply not a necessary part of speaking in tongues."[2] While some critics of the tongues movement often dismiss it as "praying in gibberish," its defenders point to the results of the study done by Morton T. Kelsey, a disciple of Jung:

> It seems to be a physical impossibility to duplicate tongue-speech by deliberate imitation; when gibberish is produced by conscious effort, this also produces muscular tension which soon differentiates the sounds from the effortless flow of glossolalia.[3]

These observations point to the mounting difficulties separating those pro and con. Obviously, both the defenders of glossolalia and the remainder of Christendom must share the burden of compromise if these difficulties are to be overcome.

[2]Morton T. Kelsey, *Tongue Speaking: An Experiment in Spiritual Experience* (Garden City, New York: Doubleday, 1964), p. 145.

[3]*Ibid.,* p. 6.

a. A reconstructed non-Pentecostal position. The apostle Paul wrote this: "So, my brethren, earnestly desire to prophesy, and do not forbid speaking in tongues; but all things should be done decently and in order" (I Cor. 14:39-40). Thus, while Paul does advocate certain legislative controls for the exercise of glossolalia, he does not forbid the phenomenon among the Corinthian Christians. Can the church today have a different attitude? Paul does, however, recommend that the Christians at Corinth seek a more important gift — prophesying (I Cor. 14:39). Here, Paul probably meant the intelligent expression of the reality and power of God and of his redemptive work and purposes among men. Even though Paul ranks glossolalia low among spiritual gifts, he nonetheless does consider it a gift. It would appear, therefore, that the task of the non-Pentecostal Christian with respect to his Pentecostal brother is three-fold: (1) Accept glossolalia as a legitimate, nonnormative experience which attests to the presence of God's Spirit. (2) More importantly, accept the brother who speaks in tongues, even if he is unwilling to search elsewhere for a more meaningful symbol through which to express his conviction that God's Spirit is working in and through him. The person who clings to this traditional symbol needs as much to be accepted as any other Christian. (3) Admit that important lessons and insights can be learned from the Pentecostals. The structure of glossolalia is a loud protest to the sometimes cold, impersonal form which institutional worship may acquire. Indeed, some regard the movement as a rebellion against over-intellectualized and over-organized Christianity. Further, the Pentecostals have demonstrated a zeal and commitment to the Christian faith that is matched only by a small minority of denominations. This may be because they have set definite spiritual goals and have worked out highly developed methods by which to reach these goals. Regardless of how nonparticipants view the outward manifestations of glossolalia, only the most narrow-minded Christian would proceed to write off the Pentecostal denominations as insignificant and irrelevant.

b. A reconstructed Pentecostal position. Alternatively, the Pentecostal advocates of glossolalia as an objective phenomenon must lend a sympathetic ear to those who are skeptical of the worth of random speech sounds as a valid symbol of the presence of God's Spirit. The serious glossolaliac who is concerned about meaningful dialog with his non-Pentecostal brother might consider the following suggestions: (1) Recognize that while glossolalia is *a* legitimate symbol it is not the only symbol of the presence of God's Spirit, and consequently it is not normative for all Christendom. The Christian whose world-view requires him to reject the symbol of speaking in tongues may not be passing a judgment upon his Pentecostal brother at all; rather, he may be honestly searching elsewhere for what to him is a more meaningful symbol through which to express his belief that God is dwelling in him. The Pentecostal must not view as a threat the estimate of glossolalia that relegates it to the place of irrationalism. One individual who spoke in tongues described the experience as follows:

> I heard of a group of people . . . who had a dynamic experience of the Spirit and manifested the gifts of tongues. I was filled with question, being a rather conservative person and of a rather intellectual bent, but I was more filled with an awareness that these people really had something vital in their Christian living that I needed and wanted. So I took the leap and joined their group . . . earnestly seeking the Holy Spirit and whatever gifts he might want to give me. [The] willingness to receive the gift of tongues was a real turning point, because that willingness — to be a fool for Christ — involved a new degree of surrender, which made it possible for the Spirit to come. Needless to say, he did come in great overwhelming power and joy. . . .[4]

In this case history, as in many others, the symbol is relatively unimportant, while the total surrender is absolutely necessary and all-important. Thus, the glossolaliac should allow his non-Pentecostal brother a certain degree of freedom in choosing other symbols that will be as meaningful for him as glossolalia is for the Pentecostal. What

[4]Quoted in Fred B. Morris, "Now I Want You All to Speak in Tongues . . .", *The Christian Advocate,* VII (July 4, 1963), 9-10.

symbols are there from which the non-Pentecostal can choose? Perhaps this total surrender could be symbolized through specific involvement with minority groups who seek equal housing and job opportunities; through commitment to the cause of Christian unity around the world; or through leadership in the Christian understanding of war, of sex, or of leisure time.

(2) Not only must the glossolaliac recognize that tongue-speaking is not the only evidence of the indwelling of God's Spirit, but he must avoid stating or implying that glossolalia is superior to all other gifts. The words of Paul are clear:

> Now there are varieties of gifts, but the same Spirit; and there are varieties of service, but the same Lord; and there are varieties of working, but it is the same God who inspires them all in every one. To each is given the manifestation of the Spirit for the common good. To one is given through the Spirit the utterance of wisdom, and to another the utterance of knowledge according to the same Spirit, to another faith by the same Spirit, to another gifts of healing by the one Spirit, to another the working of miracles, to another prophecy, to another the ability to distinguish between spirits, to another various kinds of tongues, to another the interpretation of tongues. (I Cor. 12:4-10)

Larry Christenson, pastor of the Trinity Lutheran Church in San Pedro, California, has had extensive experience with tongue-speech, and he maintains that the experience of glossolalia is only *one* gift of the Spirit. In fact, Christenson continues, the Pentecostal does not pray for the gift of tongues, but rather for the gift of the Holy Spirit. Those who have not received this specific gift, therefore, should not be regarded as inferior by the glossolaliacs, nor should the former reject the latter because they have found meaning in tongue-speech. His central conclusion for the church today is that glossolalia is a valuable experience — one that should not be forbidden. He asks Christian love and understanding from those who have not had this experience as well as from those who have, as each seeks to relate to the other.

Finally (3) a glossolaliac must realize that to reject

glossolalia is not perforce to reject the belief that the Holy Spirit has a place in the life of an individual. Many non-Pentecostals know that the Holy Spirit is active and powerful, but expect the Spirit to manifest himself not in spectacular demonstrations but rather in the Christian graces mentioned in Galatians 5:22-23a.

Pentecostals and non-Pentecostals alike must exercise Christian love as they seek to examine the other's estimate of the external form of glossolalia. Each group has its differing estimates of the significance of this outward manifestation of the Spirit's presence. Perhaps more light can be shed upon the problem by moving to a discussion of the *meaning* of this phenomenon.

B. The Symbolism of Glossolalia

In terms of its objective form, glossolalia cannot be said to be a religious phenomenon per se, since phenomena identical in sound and psychological effect can occur in a nonreligious context; therefore, the inherent meaning of the phenomenon must transcend its formal structure. What, then, did this symbol *mean,* and what should it signify in the church today?

1. The Meaning of Biblical Glossolalia

The Pentecost event very definitely made a tremendous impression upon all those present, as well as those who later heard of the tradition and those who read of it after Luke wrote Acts. In fact, the records seem to indicate that the Pentecost experience was simulated in other instances (Acts 4:31; 10:44-48; 19:2-7). At Pentecost, a soul-stirring experience dynamically affected the lives of those converts who were sensitized to and expectant of some great revelation from God. Consequently a number of those present broke forth spontaneously into ecstatic, involuntary speech. Something so greatly impressed them that it called forth an ecstasy of joy which took the form of "speaking in tongues." Peter attributed this demonstration to the action of the Holy Spirit (Acts 2:33; 2:28). Evidently, glossolalia was accepted as unquestionable evidence of possession by the Spirit of God. For the converts it was a manifestation of the inflowing of the divine Spirit — the Spirit of power. While the phenomenon was not mechanical or induced, a significant religious realization lay behind it. This experience was evidently so impressive that others, encouraged by Peter's promise of a share in such an experience, began to seek it so that they might share in the power which lay behind it.

There is little question that Luke intended his reader to understand that the converts of the Jesus-faith received the Spirit, and that this Spirit came in *power*. This indwelling of God's Spirit became the *sine qua non* of their teaching and practice (Acts 2:38). For Paul it may well have become an essential requirement — a standard for conversion and religious experience of all the followers of Jesus. His letters seem to indicate that converts not only must have the Spirit, but must also *demonstrate* their possession of it (see Gal. 5:16; 5:22; 5:23). He maintained that the Spirit was supposed to reveal his presence in the believers by special gifts, that is, the development of particular powers, gifts, and graces which could be accounted for only by the presence of God's Spirit of power. Paul offers specific lists of these gifts (I Cor. 12:10; 12:28-31). Among these is glossolalia.

Seen in this context — *a* gift of the Spirit — what did this glossolalia in Acts signify? One evident feature of the phenomenon is that the vocal sounds were addressed to God. This point should not be neglected, as it helps to indicate the meaning of glossolalia. Luke indicates that "they heard them speaking in tongues and extolling God" (Acts 10:46a). Paul points out to the Corinthians that "one who speaks in a tongue speaks not to men but to God" (I Cor. 14:2a). Probably glossolalia was not intended to convey a message to men; rather, it was a form of prayer (I Cor. 14:14; 14:16). It was an effort to express to God the inexpressible indwelling of the Spirit of God. When the truth of the *kerygma* sank home to a responsive heart, ordinary human language was too restrictive to express the depth of the emotions that were aroused; therefore, the convert broke forth in ecstatic speech. It was an objective witness to the reality of the *kerygma*. The gifts, then, are to be studied as a part of the Spirit's witness to the gospel.

2. A Critical Evaluation of the Symbolic Meaning of Glossolalia

All Christians ought to recognize that there is a relevant place for the Spirit of God in the church today. The various Pentecostal sects and others who manifest glossolalia have chosen not to suppress "speech about God." They are seeking to give meaning and content to their belief that God's Spirit moves spontaneously in the church and in individual lives. In terms of the individual, the Spirit's unique work is the endowing of the individual with specific gifts. Luke maintains, for example, that Agabus prophesied at the bidding of the Holy Spirit (Acts 11:28; 21:11). Similarly, in the context of the church, the Holy Spirit is that power which enables the church to carry out her mission. In summarizing the work of the church in Jerusalem, Luke notes that "with great power the apostles gave their testimony to the resurrection of the Lord Jesus" (Acts 4:33). This, then, was a community of power because its constituents possessed the Holy Spirit which empowered them to witness to the gospel.

Thus, the various Pentecostal groups have forced the more "respectable" denominations to take a hard look at their doctrine of the Holy Spirit. Wayne Oates feels that religion is the "delicate" subject of this generation, and that there is a certain shyness and inarticulateness when it comes to talking about God. For this reason — and others — he defends the glossolaliac:

> The person who speaks in tongues cannot be "written off" as a fanatic, a sick person, or a fool. We do not know how to pray as we ought. Therefore, these tongue speakings may be the "sighs too deep for words." On the other hand, they may become extremely meaningful to us personally whether they mean anything else to anyone else at all notwithstanding.[5]

[5]Wayne E. Oates, "A Socio-Psychological Study of Glossolalia," in Frank Stagg, E. Glenn Hinson and Wayne E. Oates, *Glossolalia: Tongue Speaking in Biblical, Historical, and Psychological Perspective* (Nashville: Abingdon, 1967), p. 77.

Moreover, in general there is a feeling among many Christians that charismatic behavior is not "respectable." Some say that the church has lost its "charisma," that men look back to it as a thing of the past. Into this spiritual vacuum the Pentecostal sects bring a needed emphasis upon the role of the Holy Spirit. Apart from affording the individual and the community meaningful channels through which to express the conviction that God's Spirit is working, the organized, institutional church with its "busyness" is irrelevant to the needs of mankind. The late James Pike was correct in his analysis:

> Proponents of this [glossolalic] movement are indubitably right that our Church is in need of a greater sense of the activity of the Holy Spirit in the here and now and a greater resultant zeal of the Mission of the Church, for a change in lives and for personal testimony to Christ.[6]

By the same token, the Pentecostal groups need to be more creative in developing and articulating a theology of glossolalia, that is, what the phenomenon *means* for the Christian life. I have suggested here that the apostles understood its significance to be that it indicated the presence of God's Spirit in the individual. A telling weakness of most Pentecostal material is that it says little or nothing about the relevance of glossolalia for the Christian life. Rather, one gets the impression that the experience per se is what is being sought. *Eternity* magazine describes how a group will gather about a seeker and lay hands on his head. The seeker will be urged to use some foreign words he knows to start the flow. In addition he might be advised to let his jaw become loose and his tongue limp. Or he might be asked to repeat the name of Jesus over and over with great rapidity until he begins to stammer. "Now you are getting it," the group will tell the seeker.

It would appear that some Pentecostals assume that a spiritual blessing *must* be attested to by means of a physical phenomenon. This is a difficult position to defend, especially when some prominent Pentecostal writers con-

---

[6]James A. Pike, "Pastoral Letter Regarding 'Speaking in Tongues,'" *Pastoral Psychology*, XV (May, 1964), 57.

cede that the tongue-speaking which occurred at Corinth had nothing directly to do with being filled with the Spirit. Paul took a different stance in Galatians: "But the fruit of the Spirit is love, joy, peace, patience, kindness, goodness, faithfulness, gentleness, self-control" (Gal. 5:22-23a. Cf. Matt. 7:22-23).

When one demands any specific physical sign as proof for any subjective experience, there will evolve an implicit standard that will rigidly separate those who possess the sign and those who do not. Such a position could be a real stumbling block to Christian unity. Explicit in some Pentecostal writers is the view that Spirit-baptism — as objectified by glossolalia — is a prerequisite to sanctification.[7]

In Christian worship there ought to be more room for spontaneity in worship — more opportunity for the worshippers to participate. Bishop Pike's remarks do not render invalid the practice of glossolalia; rather, he forbids its practice in public worship:

> While there is no inhibition whatsoever as to devotional use of speaking in tongues, I urge that there be no services or meetings in our Churches or in homes or elsewhere for which the expression or promotion of this activity is the purpose, or of which it is a part.[8]

His statement presupposes a certain rigidity in the order of service *from which there will be no deviation.* Henry P. Van Dusen has concluded:

> I have come to feel ... that the Pentecostal Movement, with its emphasis upon the Holy Spirit, is more than just another revival. It is a revolution in our day. It is a revolution comparable in importance with the establishment of the original Apostolic Church and with the Protestant Reformation.[9]

It may well be that one of the greatest needs of the modern church is to rediscover the tremendous resources

---

[7]See P. C. Nelson, *Bible Doctrine* (Springfield, Missouri: Gospel Publishing House, 1948), p. 94 and Ralph M. Riggs, *The Spirit Himself* (Springfield, Missouri: Gospel Publishing House, 1949), p. 73.

[8]Pike, p. 59.

[9]Quoted in John L. Sherrill, *They Speak with Other Tongues* (Westwood, New Jersey: Revell, 1964), p. 27.

of the Holy Spirit. All of Christendom needs to experience the joy and vigor of the Spirit's presence. Indeed, as James McCord, president of Princeton Seminary, has said:

> Ours must become the Age of the Spirit, of God active in the world, shaking and shattering all our forms and structures, and bringing forth responses consonant with the Gospel and the world's needs.[10]

Again, John Newport asks reflectively:

> Could it be that God is using the Pentecostal movement and the so-called Neo-Pentecostal or charismatic revival to summon us not to quench the Spirit and to earnestly desire and appropriate the power and resources of the Holy Spirit?[11]

Could it be that through this "strange stirring in the Church" God may be calling Christians to a higher level of faith and service?

Finally, let there be constructive dialog between the glossolaliacs and non-glossolaliacs. Let us all affirm that every Christian needs both order and freedom. Out of constructive debate could come a resolution of differences that would be profitable to all. There is a Presbyterian church in Pennsylvania, for example, where a "pray and praise" service on Saturday night precedes the more formal, liturgical worship service on Sunday morning. This pattern of worship is intended to maintain a proper balance between order and freedom. This calendar of worship does not "quench" the Spirit.

C. Conclusion

Admittedly, glossolalia often arises out of a highly emotional atmosphere. Often those who speak in tongues are ultra-conservative, and consequently the usual reaction is to write off the entire movement as the product of some kind of psychosis which comes to the surface during high-pitched revivalist meetings. Such a cursory dismissal of the

---

[10]*Ibid.,* p. 68.

[11] John P. Newport, "Speaking in Tongues," *Home Missions,* XXXVI (May, 1965), 25.

challenge of the Pentecostals, however, does not settle the question of what this new outburst of tongues means for the rest of Christendom.

Those who reject tongue-speaking as no longer relevant for the church ought to be secure enough to concede that these random speech sounds may attest to a genuine experience: namely, that God's Spirit is dwelling in the individual in power. This means that Christendom generally is obligated to accept the glossolaliac brother who is convinced that this particular symbol is adequate for him. Moreover, the non-glossolaliac — admitting that the symbol originally attested to the power and presence of God — must now search elsewhere for a relevant symbol to indicate his commitment to a belief in the Spirit's presence.

The proponents of glossolalia ought to recognize that the phenomenon had been abused in the Corinthian congregation. Paul consequently set down some rules and limits for its future use. Among the Pentecostals in this century there have been similar abuses. The former General Secretary of the Pentecostal World Conference is reported to have said:

> There is not much in church services that is more distressing than the shocking ignorance about, and the lamentable absence of the gifts of the Holy Spirit. Even in our Pentecostal Churches, where there is evidence of more liberty in the Spirit, we find far more physical and emotional "reactions" to the presence of the Spirit. . . . I consider it heresy to speak of shaking, trembling, falling, dancing, clapping, shouting, and such like actions as "manifestations" of the Holy Spirit. These are purely human reactions to the power of the Holy Spirit and frequently hinder, more than help, to bring forth genuine manifestations.[12]

Consequently, those who speak in tongues must recognize that these objections and fears are ever present and real. On the other hand, non-Pentecostals must recognize that abuses are neither necessary nor inevitable.

Likewise, the glossolaliac must not expect all Christians

[12]Tod W. Ewald, "Aspects of Tongues," *The Living Church,* CXLVI (June 2, 1963), 13.

to speak in tongues; neither must the Pentecostal deny his brother in Christ the right to search for yet another symbol to express the indwelling of God's Spirit, if that symbol would give concrete meaning to the conviction that God is dwelling in the individual.

The most important question about glossolalia for the church is this: Is glossolalia a legitimate expression of the presence of the Spirit? Paul's answer is that it is a legitimate expression if the time and place are right. Whether this is so is determined by whether love is increased or, at the very least, not harmed in any way whatsoever. This will mean that Pentecostals and non-Pentecostals alike will have to recognize that, though their methods are different, their goal is the same: to demonstrate the presence of God's Spirit.

Truly, then, the way for both those with and those without the experience to keep the phenomenon in perspective is neither to forbid nor force tongues, but rather to exercise mutual tolerance, understanding and Christian love.

BIBLIOGRAPHY

I. Books

Bach, Marcus. *The Inner Ecstasy.* Nashville: Abingdon Press, 1969.

Barnett, Maurice. *The Living Flame.* London: Epworth Press, 1953.

Bergsma, Stuart. *Speaking with Tongues.* Grand Rapids: Baker Book House, 1965.

Bresson, Bernard L. *Studies in Ecstasy.* New York: Vantage Press, 1966.

Brumback, Carl. *Suddenly from Heaven: A History of the Assemblies of God.* Springfield, Missouri: Gospel Publishing House, 1961.

Bruner, Frederick Dale. *A Theology of the Holy Spirit: The Pentecostal Experience and the New Testament Witness.* Grand Rapids: Eerdmans Publishing Company, 1970.

Cantelon, Willard. *El Bautismo en el Espíritu Santo.* Third edition. Springfield, Missouri: Editorial Vida, 1955.

Cutten, George B. *Speaking with Tongues: Historically and Psychologically Considered.* New Haven: Yale University Press, 1927.

Dalton, Robert Chandler. *Tongues Like As of Fire: A Critical Study of the Modern Tongue Movement in the Light of Apostolic and Patristic Times.* Springfield, Missouri: Gospel Publishing House, 1945.

Hoekema, Anthony A. *What About Tongue-Speaking?* Grand Rapids: Eerdmans Publishing Company, 1966.

Horton, Wade H. (ed.). *The Glossolalia Phenomenon.* Cleveland, Tennessee: Pathway Press, 1966.

Kelsey, Morton T. *Tongue Speaking: An Experiment in Spiritual Experience.* Garden City, New York: Doubleday and Company, 1964.

Kendrick, Klaude. *The Promise Fulfilled: A History of the Modern Pentecostal Movement.* Springfield, Missouri: Gospel Publishing House, 1961.

Lang, G. H. *The Modern Gift of Tongues: Whence Is It? A Testimony and an Examination.* London: Marshall Brothers, n.d.

Lombard, Emile. *De la Glossolalie chez les premiers chrétiens et des phénomènes similaires.* Lausanne: G. Bridel, 1910.

McCrossan, Thomas J. *Speaking with Tongues, Sign or Gift, Which?* New York: Christian Alliance Publishing Company, 1927.

Mackie, Alexander. *The Gift of Tongues: A Study in Pathological Aspects of Christianity.* New York: George H. Doran Company, 1921.

Martin, Ira J. *Glossolalia in the Apostolic Church: A Survey Study of Tongue-Speech.* Berea, Kentucky: Berea College Press, 1960.

Mosiman, Eddison. *Das Zungenreden geschichtlich und psychologisch untersucht.* Tübingen: J. C. B. Mohr, 1911.

Schlauch, Margaret. *The Gift of Tongues.* New York: Modern Age Books, 1942.

Sherrill, John L. *They Speak with Other Tongues.* Westwood, New Jersey: Fleming H. Revell, 1964.

Stagg, Frank, E. Glenn Hinson, and Wayne E. Oates. *Glossolalia: Tongue Speaking in Biblical, Historical, and Psychological Perspective.* Nashville: Abingdon Press, 1967.

Stolee, Haakon J. *Pentecostalism: The Problem of the Modern Tongues Movement.* Minneapolis, Minnesota: Augsburg, 1936.

II. Articles

Beare, Frank W. "Speaking with Tongues," *Journal of Biblical Literature,* LXXXIII (1964), 229-246.

Clemen, Carl. "The 'Speaking with Tongues' of the Early Church," *Expository Times,* X (1898), 344-352.

Currie, Stuart D. "Speaking in Tongues: Early Evidence Outside the New Testament Bearing on 'Glossais Lalein,'" *Interpretation,* XIX (1965), 274-294.

Davies, J. G. "Pentecost and Glossolalia," *Journal of Theological Studies,* III (1952), 228-231.

Dewar, Lindsay. "The Problem of Pentecost," *Theology,* IX (1924), 249-259.

Douglas, J. D. "Tongues in Transition," *Christianity Today*, X (July 8, 1966), 34.

Farrell, Frank. "Outburst of Tongues: The New Penetration," *Christianity Today*, VII (September 13, 1963), 3-7.

Fuller, Reginald H. "Tongues in the New Testament," *American Church Quarterly*, III (Fall 1963), 162-168.

Gundry, Robert H. "Ecstatic Utterance," *Journal of Theological Studies* (new series), XVII (October 1966), 299-307.

Henke, Frederick G. "The Gift of Tongues and Related Phenomena at the Present Day," *American Journal of Theology*, XIII (April 1909), 193-206.

Mills, Watson E. "Reassessing Glossolalia," *Christian Century*, LXXXVII (October 14, 1970), 1217-1219.

Oman, John B. "On 'Speaking in Tongues': A Psychological Analysis," *Pastoral Psychology*, XIV (December 1963), 48-51.

Pattison, E. Mansell. "Behavioral Science Research on the Nature of Glossolalia," *Journal of the American Scientific Affiliation*, XX (September 1968), 73-86.

Sadler, A. W. "Glossolalia and Possession: An Appeal to the Episcopal Study Commission," *Journal for the Scientific Study of Religion*, IV (1964), 84-90.

Samarin, William J. "Glossolalia as Learned Behaviour," *Canadian Journal of Theology*, XV (January 1969), 60-64.

Van Elderen, Bastiaan. "Glossolalia in the New Testament," *Bulletin of the Evangelical Theological Society*, VII (Spring 1964), 53-58.

III. Theses

Cheshire, C. Linwood. "The Doctrine of the Holy Spirit in the Acts." Unpublished Master's thesis, Union Theological Seminary, Richmond, Virginia, 1953.

Decker, Ralph Winfield. "The First Christian Pentecost." Unpublished Doctor's dissertation, Boston University, Boston, 1941.

Kay, Thomas Oliver. "Pentecost: Its Significance in the Life of the Church." Unpublished Master's thesis, Southern Baptist Theological Seminary, Louisville, 1954.

Lovekin, Arthur Adams. "Glossolalia: A Critical Study of Alleged Origins, the New Testament and the Early Church." Unpublished Master's thesis, University of the South, Sewanee, Tennessee, 1962.

Mills, Watson E. "A Theological Interpretation of Tongues in Acts and I Corinthians." Unpublished Doctor's dissertation, Southern Baptist Theological Seminary, Louisville, Kentucky, 1968.

Shumway, Charles William. "A Critical History of Glossolalia." Unpublished Doctor's dissertation, Boston University, Boston, 1919.

Vivier, Lincoln Morse Van Eetveldt. "Glossolalia." Unpublished Doctor's dissertation, University of Witwatersrand, Johannesburg, South Africa, 1960.

Welliver, Kenneth Bruce. "Pentecost and the Early Church." Unpublished Doctor's dissertation, Yale University, New Haven, Connecticut, 1961.

Wolfram, Walter Andrew. "The Sociolinguistics of Glossolalia." Unpublished Master's thesis, Hartford Seminary, Hartford, Connecticut, 1966.

IV. Dictionary Articles

Andrews, Elias. "Ecstasy," *The Interpreter's Dictionary of the Bible*, George Arthur Buttrick, editor. 4 vols. Nashville: Abingdon Press, 1962. A-D, 21-22.

_____. "Tongues, Gift of," *The Interpreter's Dictionary of the Bible*, George Arthur Buttrick, editor. 4 vols. Nashville: Abingdon Press, 1962. R-Z, 671-672.

Clemens, J. S. "Pentecost," *A Dictionary of the Apostolic Church*, James Hastings, editor. 2 vols. New York: Charles Scribner's Sons, 1908. II, 160-164.

Nicol, T. "Pentecost," *A Dictionary of Christ and the Gospels*, James Hastings, editor. 2 vols. New York: Charles Scribner's Sons, 1906. II, 331-334.

Putnam, W. G. "Tongues, Gift of," *New Bible Dictionary*. Grand Rapids: Eerdmans Publishing Company, 1962. P. 1286.

Rylaarsdam, J. C. "Pentecost," *The Interpreter's Dictionary of the Bible*, George Arthur Buttrick, editor. 4 vols. Nashville: Abingdon Press, 1962. K-Q, 727.

V. Encyclopedia Articles

Easton, Burton Scott. "Tongues, Confusion of," *The International Standard Bible Encyclopaedia*. 5 vols. Chicago: The Howard-Severance Company, 1915. V, 2994-2995.

_____. "Tongues, Gift of," *The International Standard Bible Encyclopaedia*. 5 vols. Chicago: The Howard-Severance Company, 1915. V, 2995-2997.

Eisenstein, J. D. "Pentecost in Rabbinic Literature," *The Jewish Encyclopedia*, Isidore Singer, editor. 12 vols. New York: Funk and Wagnalls Company, 1906. IX, 592-594.

Feine, Paul. "Speaking with Tongues," *Schaff-Herzog Encyclopedia of Religious Knowledge*. 15 vols. Grand Rapids: Baker Book House, 1960. XI, 36-39.

Magnus, J. L. "Pentecost," *The Jewish Encyclopedia*, Isidore Singer, editor. 12 vols. New York: Funk and Wagnalls Company, 1906. IX, 592.

Moorehead, William G. "Tongues of Fire," *The International Standard Bible Encyclopaedia*. 5 vols. Chicago: The Howard-Severance Company, 1915. V, 2997-2998.

Schmiedel, Paul W. "Acts of the Apostles," *Encyclopaedia Biblica*, T. K. Cheyne and J. S. Black, editors. 3 vols. New York: Macmillan and Company, 1899. I, 38-57.

"Tongues, Gift of," *Encyclopaedia Britannica*. 23 vols. Chicago: William Benton, 1962. XXII, 288-289.

VI. Denominational Publications

Arnot, Arthur B. "The Modern 'Speaking with Tongues,' " *The Evangelical Christian*, XLVI (January 1950), 23-25, 59.

Bach, Marcus. "Whether There Be Tongues," *Christian Herald*, LXXXVII (May 1964), 10-11, 20, 22.

Bennett, Dennis J. "Speaking in Tongues," *The Living Church*, CXLII (January 1, 1961), 12-13.

_____. " 'They Spake with Other Tongues and Magnified God!' " *Full Gospel Business Men's Voice*, VIII (October 1960), 6-8.

Bloesch, Donald G. "The Charismatic Revival," *Religion in Life*, XXXV (1965-1966), 364-380.

Brandt, R. L. "The Case for Speaking with Other Tongues," *Pentecostal Evangel*, XLVIII (June 5, 1960), 4, 29-30.

Cleveland, Lester D. "Let's Demythologize Glossolalia," *The Baptist Program*, XLV (June 1967), 8, 11.

Edman, Raymond V. "Divine or Devilish?" *Christian Herald*, LXXXVII (May 1964), 14-17.

Ewald, Tod W. "Aspects of Tongues," *The Living Church*, CXLVI (June 2, 1963), 12-13, 19.

Finch, John G. "God-Inspired or Self-Induced," *Christian Herald*, LXXXVII (May 1964), 12-13, 17-19.

Fowler, J. Roswell. "Holiness, the Spirit's Infilling, and Speaking with Tongues," *Paraclete*, II (Summer 1968), 7-9.

"Glossolalia," *The Living Church*, CXLVI (May 19, 1963), 11-12.

Goldsmith, Harry. "The Psychological Usefulness of Glossolalia to the Believer," *View*, II (1965), 7-8.

Gosnell, L. W. "The Gift of Tongues: The True and the False," *The Christian Workers Magazine*, XIII (November 1913), 1-11.

Hoy, Albert L. "Public and Private Uses of the Gift of Tongues," *Paraclete*, II (Fall 1968), 10-14.

Mills, Watson E. "A New Lingo for Christendom?" *Home Missions*, XLI (June 1970), 28-29.

_____. "Tongue Speech: Revolution or Renewal," *The Student*, L (November 1970), 29-31.

Morris, Fred B. "Now I Want You All to Speak in Tongues . . .", *The Christian Advocate*, VII (July 4, 1963), 9-10.

Newport, John P. "Speaking in Tongues," *Home Missions*, XXXVI (May 1965), 7-9, 21-26.

Palmer, Everett W. "Speaking in Tongues," *Christian Advocate*, VIII (October 22, 1964), 9-10.

Pike, James. "Glossolalia," *The Living Church*, CXLVI (May 19, 1963), 11.

Rice, Robert F. "Christian Glossolalia Through the Centuries," *View*, I (1964), 1-7.

VII. Popular Magazines

Bess, Donovan. " 'Speaking in Tongues' — the High Church Heresy," *Nation*, CXCVII (1962), 173-177.

"No Noisy Gongs," *America*, CXI (1964), 173-174.

"Pentecostal Tongues and Converts," *Time*, XC (July 28, 1967), 64.

Phillips, McCandlish. "And There Appeared to Them Tongues of Fire," *The Saturday Evening Post*, CCXXXVII (May 16, 1964), 31-32, 38-40.

"Taming the Tongues," *Time*, LXXXIV (July 10, 1964), 64-66.

Tinker, Frank A. "The Strange Words That Threaten Protestant Unity," *Pageant*, XX (June 1965), 80-85.

"Worship: Blue Tongues," *Time*, LXXXI (March 29, 1963), 52.

VIII. Reports and Papers

Campbell, J. A. "A Speaking Acquaintance with Tongues." Unpublished paper, University of Pittsburgh, 1965.

"The Diocese of Chicago's Report on Spiritual Speaking," *The Living Church*, CXLIV (January 1, 1961), 10-11, 18.

Lester, Andrew D. "Glossolalia: A Psychological Evaluation." Unpublished paper, Southern Baptist Theological Seminary, Louisville, 1965.

Nida, Eugene. "Preliminary Report on Glossolalia." A paper presented at the Linguistic Society of America, New York, December, 1964.

Oates, Wayne E. "Ecstaticism." Unpublished seminar paper, Duke University, Durham, North Carolina, 1943.

"Preliminary Report." Unpublished paper, Division of Pastoral Services of the Episcopal Diocese of California, Study Commission on Glossolalia, 1963.

IX. Glossolalia-Orientated Periodicals

Abundant Life. Tulsa, Oklahoma: Oral Roberts Evangelistic Association, 1947ff.

Charisma Digest. Los Angeles: Full Gospel Business Men's Fellowship International, 1968ff.

Full Gospel Business Men's Voice. Los Angeles: Full Gospel Business Men's Fellowship International, 1953ff.

Trinity. Van Nuys, California: Blessed Trinity Society, 1962-1966.

View: A Quarterly Journal Interpreting the World-Wide Charismatic Renewal. Los Angeles: Full Gospel Business Men's Fellowship International, 1966-1968.

INDEX OF PERSONS AND AUTHORS

INDEX OF BIBLICAL REFERENCES